SALES
STRATEGIES

THE AUTHOR

Chris Newby was born in Peterborough in 1947. He was educated at Forest School and the University of Reading, where he read Cybernetics. On graduating, he joined IBM and remained there for twenty-five years, initially as a systems engineer, then salesman and product manager, and subsequently in senior positions in sales, marketing and business management.

In 1993, he left IBM to set up his own consultancy, Newbytes, which offers sales advice and training to executives from some of the world's leading organizations. He has an MBA from the Open University Business School, and is a Member of the Chartered Institute of Marketing and the Association of MBAs.

Chris lives in Winchester with his wife, Janice. They have a daughter and a son. His hobbies include mountain walking, sailing, supporting Southampton football team and playing club chess.

SALES STRATEGIES

Negotiating and Winning Corporate Deals

CHRIS NEWBY

Foreword by JOHN BOTTEN

Commercial Director of IBM United Kingdom Ltd

**KOGAN
PAGE**

The masculine pronoun has been used throughout this book. This stems from a desire to avoid ugly or cumbersome language, and no discrimination, prejudice or bias is intended.

First published in 1998

Reprinted 1999

Kogan Page Limited
120 Pentonville Road
London N1 9JN
UK

Kogan Page Limited
163 Central Avenue, Suite 4
Dover, NH 03820
USA

British Library Cataloguing in Publication Data
A CIP record for this book is available from the British Library.
ISBN 0 7494 2773 6

Typeset by Saxon Graphics Ltd, Derby
Printed and bound in Great Britain by Biddles Ltd, Guildford and King's Lynn

CONTENTS

■ Contents ■

■ *Contents* ■

ACKNOWLEDGEMENTS

In writing this book, I have been helped and encouraged by many people.

Some of the areas touched on are specialist topics in their own right, and I am greatly indebted to many people for offering me their advice and suggestions. It is impossible to name everyone, but I am particularly grateful to the following, who acted as critical readers and advisers on different parts of the text:

John Botten, MBA is the Commercial Director for IBM UK Limited. He has been a powerful influence and a good friend for many years. During my time in IBM we spent many long hours working on major deals for the firm. He has spent the last ten years negotiating, trouble-shooting and re-negotiating deals for major IT projects. He has provided me with much valued advice, especially on deal-shaping and negotiation.

Geoff Galliver, MBA CEng MIEE, of Davies, Galliver Associates, has had extensive experience in electronics, and has held senior positions in Fairchild, Tektronix and Eaton. He initiated a European start-up for LTX. He now runs his own consultancy and is an associate lecturer at the Open University Business School. Geoff introduced me to game theory.

Mike McDonald is a leading International Sales Trainer. For the last twenty years he has run Sales School, a sales training consultancy specializing in complex selling to large organizations. His early career was with IBM and Olivetti. I have learnt a great deal from working with him in recent years.

David Simpson is a partner with Andersen Consulting. He has spent his business life consulting to the financial services industry. We have worked together on several major sales campaigns in recent years. David was particularly helpful with regard to some of the global aspects of selling complex deals; he also recommended improvements to descriptions of some of the processes.

David Smith, another ex-IBM colleague, now runs his own consultancy, David Smith Associates. When I first started my own company, he gave me a lot of useful advice, and we worked together training aspiring salesmen to use many of the ideas described in this book. I am indebted to him for his help at this time, and also for the encouragement he and his wife Hilary gave me to keep writing this book.

Dr James Thompson, BA PhD Dip Clin Psychol, FBP and S, is a senior lecturer in psychology at the University of London. We have worked together on many occasions over recent years. I am grateful to him for reviewing my use of the psychological models and techniques described.

Last but not least, thanks are due to my wife, Janice. She has always backed me in all my endeavours, and the writing of this book was no exception. She was always there when I needed her, as a source of support and encouragement.

To these, and to all the others who have encouraged, cajoled and supported me in the writing of this book, my sincerest thanks are due.

FOREWORD

When Chris Newby called and offered to take me to lunch – I should have guessed! He and I met more years ago than either of us would admit to. At the time, I headed up the IBM Large Computer System operation for EMEA (Europe, Middle East and Africa) and Chris was the Product Manager for the UK.

Since Chris and I parted company as business colleagues we have maintained contact socially, and remained good friends – despite the fact that on occasion he may advise his clients on how best to negotiate with me! At the outset of our relationship we rapidly became kindred spirits. His creativity knew no bounds, as he enlisted my support in changing the way we conducted our business in the light of ever-intensifying competition. He and I share a love of doing deals which will probably endure until our dying day.

When Chris moved to pastures new, he applied his great experience to advising large companies on how to negotiate "win/win" deals – for my part, I continued to negotiate large deals in my capacity as Commercial Director for IBM in the UK. The difference between Chris and me is that as he gained further experience, he spotted a niche in the business book market, namely: a guide to complex deals written in plain English, by someone who had actually done it.

So, I agreed to spend two weeks of my holiday proofreading the draft – for the price of a lunch! Furthermore, I was then talked into writing a foreword – and as yet no lunch. As you read this book, you will find no ploys. Chris learnt to negotiate in a hard school where the company's code of conduct severely punished unethical behaviour. This not only stands him apart from most writers who seek to teach negotiation – it is also testimony to the fact that people buy from people: people they trust, relate to and, above all, where the business relationship is likely to extend way beyond the deal of the moment.

I am sure the reader will enjoy reading this as much as I did; at least I didn't have to pay for my copy.

John Botten
Commercial Director
IBM United Kingdom Limited

PREFACE

I joined IBM as a systems engineer in 1968. I recall my university tutor advising me that IBM would inevitably attempt to turn me into a salesman at the first possible opportunity. It was said more in sadness than in hope. He gave the impression that it was not really a career of which he approved.

His fears proved well founded. Within five years I had become a corporate salesman for the world's largest information technology corporation. At the age of twenty-five, I was negotiating major computer contracts with the Ministry of Defence. I found it exciting and challenging. I loved it.

Thirty years later, my enthusiasm has not diminished. Corporate selling is one of the most invigorating and rewarding professions a young person can enter. It offers tremendous opportunities for meeting all sorts of people, and for travelling the world.

It is also a demanding profession, requiring energy and commitment. It is at the cutting edge of any successful business. It demands the mastery of a surprisingly large number of skills that come naturally to a gifted few, but require much work and effort for more ordinary mortals. Good selling in the corporate environment is about effective communication. It is about thinking through a campaign strategy, selecting playing fields for each encounter, and identifying friends and enemies within the client's organization. It is about technique – listening, questioning, objection handling. It is about watching people, understanding their personality, interpreting their actions, thinking through what their motives might be. And, above all, it is about developing and sustaining long-term business and personal relationships, to the mutual benefit of both client and vendor.

This book is about selling complex deals – the multi-million dollar contracts that underpin the performance of many of the world's largest companies. After running tutorials and workshops on managing sales campaigns, I have frequently been asked by my students whether I could recommend a suitable text for further study. Libraries and bookshops are full of texts on selling technique, but I have not yet found one that covers the full cycle of sales strategies, from opportunity selection to managing the sales campaign, from shaping the deal to negotiating the contract.

This book endeavours to fill that gap. It offers some insight and guidance on the strategic capabilities a salesman needs to master if he or she is to succeed in a corporate environment.

I hope you enjoy reading it as much as I have enjoyed writing it.

Chris Newby

INTRODUCTION

'Where shall I begin, please your Majesty?' he asked.
'Begin at the beginning,' the King said, gravely, 'and go on till you come to the
end: then stop.'

Alice's Adventures in Wonderland
Lewis Carroll (1832–98), writer and mathematician

COMPLEX DEALS

The pace of change in modern business has never been greater.

Whole industries are having to change just to survive. Change is driven not by the fact that a solution or product does not work, but by competitive pressure to be at the leading edge. Past performance is no guarantee of future success. Point-of-sale systems in supermarkets are continuously being upgraded and enhanced to improve speed and efficiency at the checkout. The insurance industry has largely switched from being high-street based to telephone-based, offering improved accessibility, more rapid service and cost improvements to the customer. Many people never talk to their bank manager these days: the vast majority of customer-bank transactions are now performed through a hole in the wall.

The need for companies to remain competitive has led to a demand for services from companies that provide business solutions. Global and nationally based services firms offer knowledge capital and skilled resources to help companies effect change in order to stay on the leading edge. Technology-providers continue to innovate and devise ever more creative ways of addressing new business problems. Outsourcing companies specialize in taking over their clients' non-core processes: these can vary from running the office canteens to managing the payroll, from taking over the computer division to the provision of property-management services. The client company is then able to focus on managing its own core competencies.

These solution-providers are participating in, and influencing, the race for survival in the next millennium. They are oiling the wheels of change, helping their customers transform in order to adapt to an ever-changing external environment. They are enablers of business change. And they themselves are competing with each other in an increasingly aggressive market, constantly striving to bring more efficient and innovative solutions to their clients. If these organizations are to continue to succeed, they need not only to provide services that deliver business benefits to their corporate clients, but also to be able to sell the complex solutions they are capable of delivering in a language their clients understand.

This book is about strategies for selling complex deals.

Complex deals are agreements between two or more parties. They always involve multiple decision-makers on the buyer (or client) side, and will usually involve more than one supplier. There will frequently be more than one buying company, too. The business risks involved for buyers and vendors are generally high. There is usually a contract to define the responsibilities of each party to the deal. A complex deal will usually exceed a million dollars; in fact, typically it will be worth many millions of dollars. Large complex deals – or 'megadeals' – can run to a billion dollars or more, and will usually relate to several countries, or more than one continent.

In every industry, every year, thousands of complex deals are struck. The deals involved in, say, refurbishing an office block, buying a fleet of company cars, or procuring a consignment of laptop computers can all exceed a million dollars. A consulting contract to implement a new business process can, typically, cost ten million dollars. When IBM Global Services became strategic provider of IT services for Cathay Pacific Airways, the nine-year deal was valued at $150 million. When Citibank outsourced its data networks to AT & T Solutions, it signed a contract for $250 million. When Dupont outsourced its information technology infrastructure to Computer Sciences Corporation, the contract exceeded £3 billion. In one quarter in 1997, EDS signed two contracts worth £3.8 billion and £4.8 billion, with BellSouth Communications, and the Commonwealth Bank of Australia respectively. Defence contracts frequently run to many billions of dollars.

Large complex deals are an everyday part of modern business life.

WINNING THE DEAL

Winning a complex-deal contract requires the buyer and seller successfully to navigate three different processes. These are as follows:

❑ the buying-decision process;
❑ the deal-shaping process;
❑ the contract-negotiation process.

COMPLEX DEALS
LARGE
COMPLEX
INVOLVE MULTIPLE DECISION-MAKERS
USUALLY HIGH-RISK
MAY INVOLVE MULTIPLE SUPPLIERS
MAY INVOLVE MULTIPLE CLIENTS
OFTEN MULTI-NATIONAL
CONTRACT

Figure 0.1 depicts a fairly typical sequence of events in a competitive sales campaign, although in reality they are rarely as well ordered and predictable as the chart implies. Heavily contested sales campaigns are a blend of action and reaction to events. Often, activities do not occur precisely when expected, in the sequence they should, or at the optimal time. Effective improvisation, rather than an ability to follow rigid processes, is a quality that distinguishes many of the best sales strategists.

With that proviso, a typical sales campaign might follow the following sequence of events:

THE BUYING DECISION

The buying-decision process starts as soon as a business opportunity is identified. Opportunity identification is usually, but not always, done by the client. Sometimes, the opportunity will be no more than the germ of an idea in one executive's mind. At other times, the client will build a full internal business case in order to implement a business solution, and then approach potential suppliers for help. Occasionally, a supplier will submit an unsolicited proposal to a client for implementation of a business solution.

After identification of the opportunity, there will usually be an exchange of information on both sides – the client explaining the business need; potential suppliers outlining their ideas and capabilities. Following this exchange, suppliers will be invited to tender a solution to address the opportunity, and each will have to decide whether or not to bid. This activity is sometimes called 'opportunity qualification'; *see* Chapter 1 for more on this.

Once a vendor has decided to bid for a contract, understanding where the power lies within the client organization is of paramount importance. Building relationships with those who will make the vendor decision, as

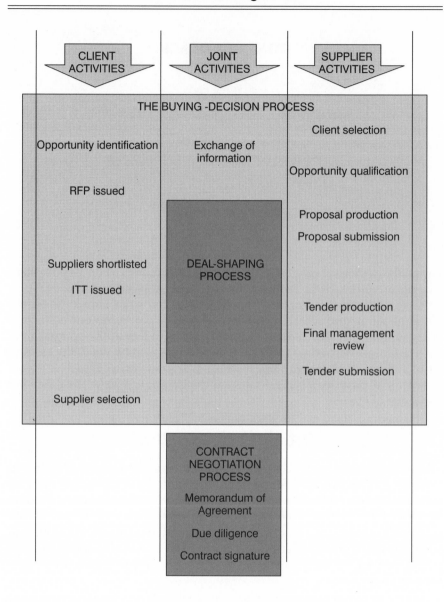

Figure 0.1: *Examples of the processes and sub-processes in a typical complex deal sales campaign*

well as with those who will influence it, can make the difference between winning and losing a deal. Chapter 2 looks at the structure of different organizations, and where power lies within them. It also looks at different types of power that executives wield within organizations, and how that power can be turned to the seller's advantage when effectively mobilized.

This book has a consistent theme. Simply stated, this is that strong relationships with the client are the most powerful basis for winning complex-deal business. Chapters 3 and 4, 'Client Relationships' and 'Selling Behaviour', discuss how salesmen may improve relationships with their clients by adapting their own behaviour.

The buying process for large bids is usually formal, and may be bureaucratic. This has traditionally been the case with Government procurements, but is now also the case with larger organizations in the private sector. Firms such as TPI, who specialize in advising their clients on the management of major procurements, are commonplace in the USA, and are increasingly being used in other parts of the world. Their usual approach is to implement a detailed and comprehensive evaluation of each supplier's offerings through a structured evaluation process.

The more formal part of the buying decision will generally be started by the client issuing an RFP ('request for proposal'). This will typically be a fairly detailed document, defining what the client wants, and the criteria by which the responses will be evaluated. Occasionally, receipt of an RFP will be the first time a supplier hears about an opportunity, although many organizations now refuse to bid for work if they have not been involved in discussions prior to the issue of the RFP.

Following evaluation of the proposals, the client will usually reduce the number of suppliers to a few short-listed competitors. Occasionally, if one supplier submits an outstanding proposal, all other proposals will be eliminated, and that supplier will be offered the contract uncontested. More usually, the short-listed vendors will receive an invitation to tender (ITT) their solutions. Tenders generally include fairly detailed solution implementation plans and prices.

The buying-decision process ends with the selection of a vendor by the client. Often, at this stage a letter of intent will be issued to the selected bidder. The other bidders will be advised that their tender has not been selected.

Managing a sales campaign whilst the client is making the buying decision is a complex task. Chapters 5, 6 and 7, 'Positioning Strategy', 'Relationship Strategy' and 'Situation Management', provide the salesman with a sales management 'tool-kit'. Chapter 8 looks at strategies for improving communication with the client.

DEAL-SHAPING

Suppliers wishing to contest a complex deal will usually be required to submit a proposal in response to an RFP. In order to do this, they will need to understand a great deal about the client organization, and its needs and aspirations. To achieve this, each supplier will begin a second activity parallel with the buying-decision process – the deal-shaping process.

Deal-shaping brings together the major factors in the seller's proposition, and explores the possible outlines – technical, contractual and financial – of the total solution. The start and end points of deal-shaping are not precisely defined. It will usually start well before proposals are submitted, and will need to be well advanced by the time tenders are submitted. It is an iterative process between supplier and buyer, critical to the overall selling process, and is discussed in more detail in Chapter 9, 'Deal-shaping'.

CONTRACT NEGOTIATION

The negotiation process relates to the drawing up of a formal agreement or contract between the selected vendor and the client. During this phase of the selling process, the vendor and client enter into detailed discussions, aimed at defining each one's own objectives, and negotiating them into an agreement.

Often, both sides will want to start on the real work of solution delivery before the lawyers have had time to draw up formal contracts. One way of allowing this to happen is to draw up a much simpler outline agreement, or 'Memorandum of Agreement'. This agreement will typically outline the major principles that both sides have agreed upon as a basis for building a contract. It will make provision for remuneration of the supplier, if appropriate, during the period between the start of solution delivery and the signing of the formal contract.

Following the signing of a 'Memorandum of Agreement', both sides, and frequently their lawyers too, will sit down to negotiate the content, and then the wording of a detailed contract. This is a critically important time, as profit margins can be won and lost during a negotiation. The process usually continues with 'due diligence', where each side makes sure that it understands what the other side is offering, and the minutiae of the contractual terms are agreed. The negotiation phase usually ends with the signing of a contract between the prime contractor and the buyer. In the event of the prime contractor using multiple suppliers, there will also be contracts between the prime contractor and its suppliers. Chapters 10, 11 and 12 are devoted to negotiation: 'Negotiation Theory' looks at the underlying game theory principles at play in any negotiation;

'Negotiation Practice' discusses the operational considerations a salesman should take into account in a negotiation; 'Negotiation Ploys' covers some of the tricks of the trade a salesman needs to be aware of before entering into a head-to-head with a client.

Chapter 13, 'Final Thoughts', looks at changes that are occurring in the role of the complex-deal salesman.

CASE STUDY – INTERNATIONAL CONSULTING AND THE GLOBAL LIFE INSURANCE COMPANY

Throughout the book, a single case study is used to illustrate the sales processes and tools described, and to give a practical counterpoint to the theory discussed.

'We', the selling organization throughout, are International Consulting, a fictional medium-sized consultancy specializing in the provision of consultancy services to the insurance sector. International Consulting is a partnership with a turnover of $50 million per year. It has twenty equity partners located in offices in the USA, UK and Australia. A small office has recently been opened in Moscow. Our core competencies are change management and information technology systems work. We have a good reputation for delivering projects on time, and to budget. However, our presence within the industry is restricted to small- and medium-sized insurance companies. We have yet to break into one of the world's top ten insurance companies, which all use the larger consultancies for their change management. We have no client base outside the insurance sector.

Global Life, another fictional organization, is a medium-sized insurance company. It provides both life- and general-insurance policies and turnover is split approximately equally between these two areas. Group turnover was $2 billion last year. The company has a market capitalization of $6 billion, and last year grew by just over 10 per cent.

We have worked with Global Life in the past on minor projects, but not within the last two years. Accordingly, we have a few relationships with the more long-serving managers in the firm. However, the company has a new dynamic management team, brought in two years ago to revitalize the firm. Its recent performance has impressed investment fund managers, who have pushed its stock price up more than 50 per cent over the past six months. Global Life has consolidated its worldwide IT operations at a major data centre in London. This centre is connected to two smaller computer centres in Dallas, Texas, and Sydney, Australia.

A simplified organization chart for Global Life is shown in Figure 0.2, showing the structure of the firm's senior management.

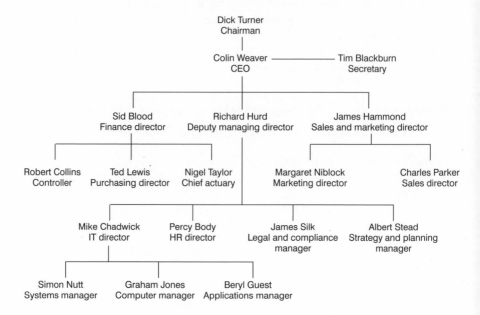

Figure 0.2: *Global Life's organization chart*

THEME

Throughout this text, there is an underlying theme – good working relationships with the client are critically important to the winning of complex deals.

Complex deals operate across important areas of the business. In a risky, mission-critical long-term contract, clients need to be able to trust the people with whom they are working. When two or more organizations enter into a complex deal, the most important factor is whether they have a relationship strong enough to deliver a solution. Any major project goes through some turbulent times. To get through them requires a good working relationship, with mutual trust. Any deal where there is suspicion between the parties is likely to be plagued by finger-pointing disputes, recriminations, and the apportioning of blame. The better the communication between the buying and selling organizations, at all levels, the better the chances of winning the sale. The successful salesman will always endeavour to establish close business and personal relationship with the key players in the client organization.

As a rider to this theme, if a close relationship can be established with the person at the top, it will make selling to the rest of the organization that much easier. Getting to see the chief executive officer (CEO) is seldom easy, but, for a large deal, what we have to say should be of real interest to him. For a deal of a significant size, the CEO will often be the final arbiter in the decision, whatever the formal decision-making process. By establishing a relationship at the top, we still may not win the sale, but we will at least have given ourselves a fighting chance.

1

CLIENT AND OPPORTUNITY SELECTION

Although a company may have a top-notch sales-force, if salesmen aren't selling the right products and services to the right customers, their energy counts for little . . .

From Sales Obsession to Marketing Effectiveness
Philip Kotler

INTRODUCTION TO PORTFOLIO MANAGEMENT

Every supplier is different. Every supplier has its strengths and weaknesses. In the same way, every client is different, and has different requirements. As a result, different buying organizations will make different buying decisions, even when considering the same choice of suppliers. Similarly, different vendors may bid significantly different solutions to the same buyer's requirement. Mapping capability to requirement, and finding the closest fit, is a responsibility of both buyer and seller. In most cases, when a sale results, a good fit will work to the benefit of both parties.

However, successful supplier companies are increasingly adding a further dimension to these considerations – the composition of their own client portfolio. At the start of every sales campaign, they are beginning to ask such questions as the following:

❑ 'Do I want to do business with this client?'
❑ 'Does this work make sense in the context of my business portfolio?'

The following real-life example is a good illustration. A German consultancy firm had hundreds of small clients, many of whom demanded a lot of selling effort, but were signing only small contracts. To improve profitability, the consultancy made a decision to take on only those clients who bought jobs in excess of 5 million dollars per contract. This decision was a conscious step towards altering the make-up of the firm's portfolio of business, and led to it turning down perfectly good business that it was well equipped to perform. Within a year, the consultancy's profitability had trebled.

Any company needs to understand the type of business it is in, or wishes to be in. Some companies call this their vision, or long-term strategy. In an ideal world, it serves to align the actions of all members of the work-force, from the chairman to new recruits. It is important, because decisions are made at all levels within all companies, and those decisions will be more effective if they are consistent and mutually compatible. The production director may decide what new products to make on a new manufacturing line, the sales director, where to open a new branch office, the salesman, which clients to pursue for new business. At each level within the decision-making process, there will be choices to be made. Demand will often exceed resources at every level. The corporate salesman needs to understand where his company wants to be, as this will influence where he spends his time, and where he deploys most effort.

CLIENT SELECTION

Portfolio management is an imprecise science, with many pitfalls. However, an attempt to manage the type of business the company wishes to be in can lead to spectacular business results. One way of considering whether to sell to a potential client is to look at its position on the sales opportunity matrix, *see* Figure 1.1. This chart is based on the premise that any company will have a mixture of sales opportunities, and will need to select which of those opportunities it can afford to contest.

A firm may have a number of established and loyal clients who place regular repeat business with it. Here, the win chance will be deemed to be high. Let us suppose that these clients provide a healthy stream of profitable business, and have a successful and productive business relationship with the supplier. Such clients, depicted in the top left-hand box, are 'prime'. These clients are attractive and should be nurtured. Many organizations employ account managers to achieve this, only bringing in front-line salesmen when major new sales opportunities are presented. Account managers are typically expected to ensure that relationships are maintained between the vendor and the client organizations. Usually, there will be no major incentive element to their remuneration package, although they may be offered a small financial incentive to grow business from existing contracts within the client organization.

It will normally not be appropriate to compromise over existing volume discount margins for these 'prime' clients. They are the bread-and-butter clients of most companies, delivering profitable day-to-day

Sales opportunity matrix

Opportunity attractiveness

	High	Low
High win chance	Prime Bid for business	Future Potential investment case
Low win chance	'Sales cost' Investment case	Worst Decline

Figure 1.1: *Sales opportunity matrix*

business, which is partly used to fund sales efforts for the investment cases. If standard terms cannot deliver to these clients, there may be something wrong with the standard terms!

Clients represented by the top right-hand box are those whose business we know we can win, although we believe it will not be that attractive to us. In these cases, an investment decision needs to be made. Much will depend upon why these clients are deemed unattractive. They may be firms that offer future potential for us, but whose potential today is small. Depending upon how stretched our resources are, and our assessment of the probability of being able to capitalize on the increased opportunity in the future, we may decide to ignore the opportunity.

It may, however, be worth establishing a good working relationship with such companies at this early stage; having a presence now may lead to exciting business in the future. Look at the example of Microsoft, a minnow in the mid-1980s, but, by the mid-1990s, one of the world's major corporations. Becoming a supplier to the mid-1980s Microsoft may have seemed much less attractive than being a supplier to them today. However, those 'early birds' are now in a position of strength, and dislodging incumbent suppliers today is undoubtedly significantly more difficult than it would have been in 1985. That German consultancy company looking to do business only with firms offering them large jobs might well have overlooked Microsoft in 1985; today, their difficulty in breaking into supplying the company could be blamed on the decisions they took at that time.

The present and future potential of the clients represented by the bottom left-hand box is there for all to see. The problem here is that everyone wants to sell to them. Typically, they are large blue chip companies, such as General Motors, Unilever or Citibank. It is here that competition can be fiercest, and heavy amounts of sales effort may be required to establish or retain a presence in these clients. It may be necessary to compromise on profit margins to win over these clients, in order to establish a base for future growth. These clients need heavy cultivation.

In the bottom right-hand quadrant lie clients who offer little attractive sales opportunity today or tomorrow; they should usually be declined. They might be low-growth or stagnant companies that do not attribute value to our core capabilities. They may have a track record of buying from our competitors.

As is apparent from a consideration of the sales opportunity matrix, there may be different reasons to invest in different types of client. It is also clear that some clients will require a different level of sales invest-ment, and that this is not necessarily proportional to the size of the busi-ness opportunity.

Apart from sales-opportunity costs, there are many other reasons why one firm might choose to decline business with another. The business risks may be too high, the firm may be a competitor, or sufficient resources may not be available to devote to the project. Every business needs to have an idea of the type of work that it wants, and of the type that it would prefer not to have. A business that does not have such a vision risks diversification into non-core activities that fail to capitalize on its key competencies.

Portfolio management is important to the corporate salesman for sev-eral reasons. First, he needs to understand where his market is. The Ford Motor Company aims for a broad market, with heavy emphasis on private and fleet buyers, calling for extensive advertising on national television and in the national press. McKinseys, the strategy consul-tancy, targets the top managements of the world's leading multi-national firms. This strategy calls for virtually no branding or mass advertising, but much development and cultivation of important relationships at senior levels. Different marketing strategies require different sales strategies.

Next, the corporate salesman needs to understand where his com-pany's core strengths are most likely to be needed. IBM in the early 1980s had a high capacity to deliver a total information technology busi-ness solution, because of the diversity of the products and services it could provide. However, at the individual product level, competitive products offering similar or superior performance at a lower price were commonplace. Several Japanese manufacturers, including Hitachi and Fujitsu, offered mainframe computers of similar architecture, but much cheaper. There were hundreds of Pacific Rim competitors manufac-turing cheaper IBM-compatible personal computers. To compete effectively in these markets, IBM put a significant amount of effort into articulating the value of having a single vendor provide all the components of a total IT solution, leveraging a core strength of product-range breadth and diversity. IBM's potential client base divided fairly quickly into those that wanted to buy cheap boxes, and those that wanted integrated business solutions. IBM was considerably more successful in selling to the latter.

The corporate salesman needs an appreciation of his own firm's strengths and weaknesses relative to the competition. I once worked for a company in Norway which was offered a large facilities-management contract, single tender. The customer had not invited a competitor to bid, yet the salesman from my company turned down the business. His view was that he was uncompetitive in this work, and that other firms could do it better and more cheaply. Whilst he could have done the job, and made some money from it, it was not the type of work that interested him, and he could not build a successful business from it. Furthermore, he took the view that, if he did the work, his long-term relationship with the client would suffer; he knew that the service he could offer would be perceived as being overpriced before the end of the contract. Instead, he sold his consultancy services to the client, and advised them on who to select for the facilities management work. His company now takes many tens of millions of kroners' worth of very profitable business from that client each year, none of it in facilities management.

There are other factors a successful corporate salesman needs to consider when selecting suitable clients. Financial measurements such as revenue, cash flow, profit and profitability are important. Adverse short-term financial problems may be the very reason that a client is seeking assistance. With the right help, a supplier might be able to share in the client's longer-term turnaround and subsequent success. However, the business risks of working with such a client may be high. Judgements on trading short- and long-term benefits are frequently crucial factors at the start of a business relationship; the corporate salesman's credibility within his own firm will often be a key determinant in their decision whether or not to proceed with business of this type. In particular, financial management, often justifiably, is prone to take a fairly sceptical view of salesmen who promise 'jam tomorrow' from a client. However, the salesman often has a broader view of the client's business and its potential in the longer term. When this is the case, it is the responsibility of the salesman to bring more strategic considerations to the debate on whether or not to pursue a specific client opportunity.

The risks involved in taking on any business should always be carefully weighed. During the 1980s, many Lloyd's 'names' lost a significant amount of money because they underestimated the risks inherent in their investments. Many firms now refuse to bid for critical elements in airline control systems – the potential consequential damages, should their equipment fail, outweigh any financial gain from supplying the equipment in the first place. Many audit firms increasingly face the prospect of litigation for failing to detect or act on management malpractice, as the Maxwell and BCCI experiences have demonstrated. Of all the factors that are considered when deciding whether or not to bid for a piece of work, risk is the one that is most regularly misjudged, overlooked, ignored or minimized.

Finally, as this book will stress throughout, strong personal and business relationships are the best way to establish and develop mutually beneficial business. It may be appropriate to take some work on, or to retreat from other opportunities, in order to preserve long-term relationships with the client.

In our case study, International Consulting does have an existing client relationship with Global Life, although it is confined very much to the old guard in Global's personnel. Although the current procurement opportunity will be competitive, it is one that plays to our competencies as an organization, and that International Consulting is well placed to win. Following the appointment of a new and aggressive top management, Global Life is the type of company International Consulting would like to work with in the future.

OPPORTUNITY SELECTION

Opportunity selection deserves careful management attention. Implementation of a formal opportunity-selection process allows the firm's senior management to review major sales opportunities. The primary objective of any selection process is to filter those opportunities the firm chooses to bid for from those it declines to contest. Service firms, in particular, have a finite capacity to take on new business, and need to be selective in the work they take on.

Selection can take place at any time during the campaign. Most firms have a formal process that allows the firm's senior management to review and approve the final deal the salesman has negotiated. For large complex deals, the supplier's senior management will usually be involved in the deal-shaping and negotiation process anyway. The factors that get reviewed at this point in the campaign are discussed in detail in Chapter 9, on deal-shaping.

Because selling complex deals is such an expensive process, many firms now implement a more general review at the start of a sales campaign, before deciding to commit significant sales resources to the campaign.

This process is referred to as 'opportunity qualification'. A qualification process typically considers a diverse range of parameters, any one of which could be an inhibitor to the supplier making a bid for a given opportunity. Such a list could include consideration of questions such as the following:

- ☐ Are we competent to bid for this opportunity?
- ☐ Do we and the client share a common vision of what is needed?
- ☐ Does the client have a business case for the opportunity?
- ☐ Is the client 'prime'?
- ☐ If the client is not prime, are there other mitigating reasons to bid for this opportunity?
- ☐ Do we have the resources necessary to deliver this opportunity? If not, can we obtain them from somewhere else?
- ☐ Do we understand the decision-making criteria that will be used in the evaluation?
- ☐ Are there any unacceptable risks to us in taking on this opportunity? If so, can they be mitigated in any way?
- ☐ How well is the scope of the opportunity defined?
- ☐ Can we work with the client and the individuals assigned to this opportunity?
- ☐ Are there any conflicts of interest in accepting this work?
- ☐ Is the opportunity too big or too small for us to bid for?
- ☐ Can we make our required profit margins on this opportunity?
- ☐ Will we have to take on any unacceptable liabilities if we win this bid?
- ☐ Does this opportunity utilize our core capabilities?
- ☐ Who are we likely to be competing against in this situation?
- ☐ What are our chances of winning if we bid for this opportunity?

In order to answer or evaluate some of these questions properly, the supplier will need to do some investigation of its own capabilities and of those of the client. For a major bid, this may take several weeks of effort. However, it will be time well spent if it leads the supplier to select the right opportunities before too much sales effort is expended.

In any internal review, the corporate salesman's instincts and advice are company assets that need to be carefully weighed alongside the functional views frequently expressed by company controllers, lawyers and sales management. The front-line salesman will be best placed to assess many of the qualification factors. Deployment of the company's sales resources towards those opportunities that best serve the firm's business vision, and play to its core competencies, can be a crucial factor in building a successful firm, based on a sound portfolio of clients.

CASE STUDY: QUALIFICATION

In our case study, Barbara Turvey, partner responsible for International Consulting, has received a letter from Global Life, indicating that Global is about to embark upon a major overhaul of their back office processes (*see* Figure 1.2).

Barbara has passed the letter to Chris Newton, a salesman who works for her. She has asked Chris to prepare an assessment of the opportunity. International Consultants has a simple qualification process for major bids. It asks its salesmen to fill in a single-sheet template summarizing the opportunity. The template invites the salesmen's comments under six major headings – Client classification, Vision, Business case, Risk assessment, Relationships and Competition. For complex bids over $5 million in value, the salesman, accompanied by the partner responsible for the client, is invited to present the situation to a management board of partners. The board comprises the managing partner, Jim Bailey, the financial controller, the company lawyer, and the head of the commercial department. Meetings to assess major new opportunities are convened as required, and are relatively informal. Figure 1.3 illustrates how Chris Newton, following several weeks of calling on different client personnel, has summarized the attractiveness of the opportunity at Global Life.

As a result of the qualification review, International Consulting's management board agrees to support bidding for the Global Life business, subject to final review immediately prior to tender submission. They recommend to Barbara Turvey that a business case should be prepared and agreed with a more senior representative for the client, cost justifying the work being requested. Whilst a letter has been issued under a director's name, Global's IT director is relatively junior. Experience with other clients has shown that, where a business case does not exist, the top management often turns the project off late in the day, and after the expenditure of many months of selling effort. Funds and headcount are authorized for the project for the duration of the sales campaign.

SALES-FORCE INCENTIVES

Results-related remuneration

For a top management with a clear business vision, ensuring that the sales-force makes decisions that are consistent with that vision is non-trivial. The purpose of an effective sales-incentive scheme is to direct the sales-force. Most sales-forces are paid by results – a combination of a base payment, and incentive or commission payments. Most salesmen enjoy the cut and thrust of a sales campaign, revelling in the risk. An element of

Mr M. Chadwick
Group IT Director
Global Life Insurance Company
1 Alpha Crescent
London

Barbara Turvey, Partner
International Consulting
1 Convent Street
London

1 September 1996

Reference ww/mc/1021/1996/pj

Dear Barbara

We are currently considering rationalization of Global Life's back-office operations, with a view to standardizing and streamlining our processes world-wide. We anticipate that we will need assistance with designing the new processes, and with the implementation of suitable IT systems to support them.

Following an initial internal debate, we are now widening our discussion to include a number of possible suppliers. We are currently entering into an informal dialogue with you and several other service-providers, with a view to inviting proposals early in the new year. We anticipate placing a contract with our chosen supplier in the middle of 1997, for an implementation of a new back office by spring 1999.

If you would like to discuss this opportunity further, please ask your representative to contact me in the first instance.

Yours sincerely,

M. Chadwick
IT Director

Figure 1.2: *Sample letter*

commission in their remuneration serves to heighten the perception of risk, and acts as an effective motivator to keep them going to the very last. A sales-force paid on commission is usually a committed sales-force.

It is, however, an unfortunate fact of modern business life that results-related systems can have a distorting effect on the behaviour of certain individuals. Revenue-incentivised sales-forces may continuously

---

Opportunity Assessment Management Summary

Date: 15 September 1996
Salesman: Chris Newton
Client: Global Life
Project duration: Start date: 2 June 1997
                        Finish date: 1 April 1999

Opportunity outline description:
Re-design and implementation of new back-office processes initially in London. Follow-on contract for a global roll out to Dallas and Sydney if successful. Contract will be for the design, build and test of new IT systems to support a new back office. The scope is wide, and embraces handling of existing business and the transition to new products.

Best estimate of key dates in procurement cycle:
RFP issued   1 November 1996
Proposal submission   16 December 1996
Short-list announced   15 January 1997
ITT issued   3 February 1997
Tender   1 April 1997
Supplier selection   1 May 1997

Estimated value: $30 million at 50 per cent gross margin

Assessment summary:
Client classification   Prime
Vision   There is some correlation of vision between us and the key evaluators. There is continuing discussion regarding the scope of the project.

Business case   No formal business case exists for this work yet. We have had a letter from Chadwick, a director, who claims that the firm is committed to the project.

Risk assessment   This is a large project for us, which will stretch our people resources, especially the change management. The scope will need tightening. The timetable will be tight. There are unlikely to be any contractual penalties for failure.

Relationships   We have good existing relationships with the client. Weaver, Hammond and Blood are strong, and want to make change happen. There may be problems with some of the longer-term employees. Nutt, the new systems manager, is supportive of our approach. There is tension between him and his boss, Chadwick. Nutt may coach us as we get to know him better.

Resources   This opportunity plays to our core strengths in change management and IT systems. We will need a large and capable implementation team, which may mean rolling some key resources off other projects, see attachments.

Competition   Bunch Computers and Taurus Consultants. Win chance 60 per cent.

Recommendation:
Proceed to RFP and submit proposal.

Figure 1.3: *Opportunity assessment management summary*

demand price cuts, and will decimate corporate margins if they are empowered to reduce prices. Profit-incentivised sales-forces may tend to focus on the immediate transaction, without regard to the longer-term reasons for investing in the client. Sales-forces not on incentive may lack the determination of their incentive-based peers.

Incentive-based sales-remuneration schemes have another major drawback. Regrettably, some salesmen will find a way to distort and beat even the most sophisticated incentive system, if it increases their commission payments. I discovered an original example of this when working with an insurance company, where the sales-force regularly used a ploy referred to as 'tombstone sales'. The company rewarded salesmen for the calls they made that resulted in a client requesting a 'Starter Pack'. Some of the insurance company's more unscrupulous salesmen would scour the obituary columns for the names of people who had recently died, find out their address, and pass the details on to the company, claiming these were individuals who had requested a Starter Pack. The company would duly dispatch the packs and pay the salesmen. There was rarely any comeback from these 'tombstone sales'. If a relative did query it, no one could prove that the deceased person had not ordered the Starter Pack immediately before dying. Over a number of years, the practice became commonplace. Abuse of its incentive system cost that insurance company many hundreds of thousands of dollars.

Another abuse of sales-incentive schemes is the year-end order rush, with which many company buyers will be familiar. Most salesmen get paid a commission for making the sale, and their sales targets are usually set to coincide with the end of the firm's financial year. Members of the sales-force who are short of their targets at the end of the year will sometimes collude with clients; an order will be raised, on the tacit understanding by both parties that it will be cancelled, before the 'delivery date', in the next financial year. This way, the salesman makes his target, and gets his commission payment.

It is easy to highlight problems with sales-compensation plans, but more difficult to make positive suggestions as to how to overcome them. No system, it seems, works perfectly in all situations. In place, then, of the 'perfect' sales-remuneration plan, I offer some guidelines for anyone attempting to build a plan. Sensibly applied, they will direct the sales-force towards winning business, without giving away the family silver.

❑ Give each salesman a clearly defined territory for which he is entirely responsible.
❑ Include a significant on-target earnings incentive element (at least 40 per cent) within the plan.
❑ Ensure that the incentive plan contains both a revenue and a profit measurement.

❏ Do not empower salesmen, or the sales organization, to alter the price of their products and services.

❏ Make all pricing adjustments subject to internal review by the financial function as well as the sales function. Ensure that the salesman's request is the starting point for any dialogue. He is closer to the action than anyone else, but may have been over-influenced by the client. He may also be obsessively keen to win the business, even if it makes him and his company little or no money.

❏ Retain the ability to add compensation to salesmen who comply with the spirit of the plan, but fall foul of an inappropriate 'rule' written to apply to a different type of behaviour.

❏ Ensure that there are processes in place to allow for client selection criteria to be overruled. Remember that every situation is unique, and there may be a good reason to chase an opportunity outside the firm's defined portfolio of selected clients.

❏ Include accelerators that encourage salesmen who have made their targets to keep going for even higher sales.

❏ Never cap a salesman's earnings for doing too well. Failure to reward salesmen for continuing to make successful sales is not just demotivating, it is unfair.

❏ Heavily punish fraudulent claims for commission.

Partnerships

Many of the world's largest deal-makers today are partnerships. Ernst and Young, for instance, is a firm with many hundreds of partners. The client partner is responsible for selling deals, and developing profitable client relationships. Partners are not on a direct incentive to sell, but participate in a profit-sharing scheme each year. This has much the same effect as an incentive system for salesmen. Each partner has an interest both in his own success and in that of his peers. Peer pressure and future career prospects within the partnership ensure that each partner stays focused on delivering profitable business to the firm.

The partnership system has its limitations, however. As a means of remunerating partners, it is focused on the short term, and can encourage risk aversion if compensating management systems are not put in place. However, it has served many of the world's largest consultancies well. Most of the major players have enjoyed spectacular growth in recent years. Not all consultancies currently implement global profit-sharing, although several of the larger ones have plans to move in that direction, as the race to support global multi-national clients intensifies. When the partner's profit pool is global, partners in each country have a vested interest in teaming with their foreign counterparts to develop multi-national clients internationally.

SUMMARY

Achieving the perfect portfolio of clients and opportunities can prove elusive. With the benefit of hindsight, there will always be business you wish you had never bothered to contest, and there will always be the ones that got away. The sales-force will never act completely predictably and not all new opportunities will come in the anticipated way. This book will not concern itself with such issues, for they are not the primary concern of the corporate salesman. From his perspective, these are long-term, esoteric considerations for the top management to worry about. The salesman's concern is with the here and now, with the action, and not with the debate. For the corporate salesman, the chase is the excitement, and the win the consummation.

For the salesman, making the sale is everything.

KEY POINTS

■ Do not chase every sales opportunity regardless of risk, size or profitability.

■ Select the type of client that the firm wishes to work with.

■ Select the right opportunities from those clients, with regard to delivering our own business objectives.

■ Select winnable opportunities that play to our own firm's strengths.

2

POWER AND DECISIONS

Nam et ipsa scientia potestas est
Knowledge itself is power

Religious Meditations, 'Of Heresies'
Francis Bacon (1561–1626), philosopher, lawyer and politician

INTRODUCTION

We had run a depressing sales campaign.

By our own assessment, we had won the technical evaluation, our price was competitive, and our terms were as good as anyone else's. Yet we had been consistently thwarted by the nominated decision-maker, the services director. He found reason beyond logic to undermine and disparage our efforts at every turn. We even suspected he might be in the pay of our competitor, his judgement seemed so biased. We knew that we would not get his recommendation at the forthcoming board meeting. The board invariably ratified his proposals. Those beneath him seemed in awe of his power, and, whilst they confided to us that they personally supported our proposals, none was prepared to oppose their boss publicly.

We held a council of war back at the office. There seemed only one course of action open to us if we were to overturn the anticipated decision – a direct appeal, over his head, to the man at the top. As the CEO of a major international company, he was a busy and powerful man He had a larger-than-life reputation for devouring subordinates. He agreed to meet us for breakfast on the day before the board meeting.

Two of us went to meet him. He was there with his personal assistant. Over toast and marmalade we presented our case to him, unemotionally, and with as much conviction as we could muster. He listened in silence for fifteen minutes, giving nothing away, but watching us intently, and occasionally nodding to signify he had understood a point that we were making. When we had finished, he said nothing initially, and leant back to reflect on what we had said. After what seemed an interminable silence, he turned to us and said sternly, 'What you are inferring is that George, for whom I have the highest regard, is about to make the wrong decision.'

Feeling there was little to gain in playing with words at this stage, I replied, 'Yes.'

He reflected for a while again, then seemed to make up his mind.

'From this meeting, I would like you to draw two lessons,' he began. 'First, if you are ever to make a success of working with us, you need to learn to work with George. In that regard, you appear to have failed so far, and that must work against you in any evaluation I make. Secondly, you did well to bring this issue to my attention before the board meeting. If we are to work together in the future, I hope you will always feel free to involve me when you judge things are going wrong in my company. Thank you for your time. You may call me tomorrow afternoon, and I will advise you of my decision.' With that, he stood, his personal assistant in tow, and left us to the remains of the coffee.

It was an impressive display of executive power. He had not given us a decision, yet he had told us so much: that he needed us to be able to work with George for him to have confidence in us; that he personally had to be seen to be supporting George; that we had, nevertheless, done the right thing in drawing his attention to a potential injustice. But most important of all, he had told us that it was to be his decision, not George's. He had told us unequivocally that, whatever happened in that board-room the following day, the decision was his. He was the real power, and he expected to be involved.

I called the CEO's office the following afternoon. The CEO had already left the office, but had left a message for me with his assistant. It read, 'George's recommendation to the board was unanimously accepted. You have won the business, and he feels confident that he can work with you to deliver a world-class solution to our problems.' The note concluded that George would be in touch shortly to open detailed contract negotiations.

We later learnt that the CEO had called George to his office immediately after our meeting. We never did find out exactly what transpired between the two men, but from then onwards, our relationship with George steadily improved, partly due to our efforts, partly due to his – but mainly due to the efforts of a shrewd and powerful CEO.

Most managers have a need for power. In his book *Understanding Organisations,* Charles Handy asserts that some degree of need for power seems to be a necessary condition for managerial success. When individuals or groups differ in their views, the relative power of the parties will determine which views prevail.

Power can take many forms, and the degree to which people elect to use the power they have will influence the way an organization makes its decisions. Understanding who has power in an organization, and the way in which that power is exercised, is important intelligence. As sales-men, we are interested, because we need to understand who has the power to make buying decisions.

Power is conditioned strongly by the context in which it is used. If we say that a boxer is powerful, we are almost certainly referring to physical capability. If we say that a bank is powerful, we are probably referring to its financial muscle and influence. If we talk about a powerful prime minister or president, we may be referring to the size of his majority or the security of his position in office. In each case, power gives someone the ability to do something, if necessary, against the wishes of someone else. However, it is obvious that a prime minister may not be very powerful in a boxing ring, and a boxer may not be the best person from whom to seek financial advice. The context in which the individual is operating influences the amount of power that individual has, and, therefore, that person's ability to persuade others.

A successful salesman has to make assessments about who has power in specific contexts. He needs to understand who will have a major say in deciding for or against his proposition, and what the boundaries of that person's responsibilities are. He needs to understand who those powerful individuals will look to for advice, and how much notice they are likely to take of it.

TYPES OF POWER

By studying the different types of power individuals may have in organizations, and the different organizational contexts within which they operate, it is possible to come up with some broad guidelines as to who is likely to be influential in specific phases of the decision-making process. From these, a sales-force can decide where to direct and expend its selling efforts most effectively.

Power within any organization can be derived in many ways: in their book *Exploring Corporate Strategy*, Johnson and Scholes list six primary sources from which the individual can derive power. These are listed on page 26.

Hierarchy

This is the power conferred on managers by their position in the organization. The formal hierarchy of power for a firm can usually be determined from the company's organization chart, with the Chairman and CEO, at its apex, the most powerful. Moving lower down the organization chart, managers at different levels have corresponding levels of hierarchical power.

JOHNSON & SCHOLES' SOURCES OF POWER

HIERARCHY
CONTROL OF STRATEGIC RESOURCES
INFLUENCE
KNOWLEDGE/SKILLS
CONTROL OF THE ENVIRONMENT
EXERCISING DISCRETION

The natural inference of hierarchies is that the more senior the manager, the greater his power. A strong relationship with the CEO can be invaluable for a salesman. If he fails to persuade any of the managers beneath the CEO, there is always a court of appeal that can overturn the decision in his favour. The converse of this is, of course, failing to establish a strong relationship with the CEO, in which case he remains vulnerable to being escalated by his competition, should the lower-level managers decide in his favour. Building relationships with the most senior manager in an organization is rarely a waste of time. Even if that person is not theoretically part of the formal decision-making process, the way the CEO is thinking can have a remarkable opinion-forming effect on the managers lower down. It takes a strong lower manager to select a solution against the clear wishes of his boss.

One of the first rules of corporate selling, therefore, is to devote as much time, effort and creative thinking as is necessary getting to see people at the top – and particularly the CEO. The salesman needs to decide who in his organization is best equipped to forge relationships at this level. Ideally, the salesman himself will form a relationship, but many senior managers high up in their own hierarchy respect hierarchy in other organizations. In this instance, the salesman will need to select from his own management someone with the appropriate seniority, responsibility and personal qualities to develop the right relationship.

Influence

Within any hierarchy, certain individuals will choose to exercise power more than others. Strong-willed or particularly opinionated managers with persuasive personal qualities may exert an influence disproportionate to their position within the hierarchy. Fast-rising managers on a top-management trajectory often carry a higher level of influence than their peers. Those around them read the writing on the wall, and, perceiving that in the future they themselves will be lower in the hierarchy, defer in anticipation. Influence can also be carried by groups or cliques. For instance, environmental pressure groups with little hierarchical authority or power have used their influence with the media, and public opinion, to bring to task major multi-national corporations, such as Shell and Exxon.

Influence may be wielded by individuals for many reasons that are not immediately apparent. Some people have great influence because they are related to the chairman, or because they have done similar work before with another organization. In one organization I knew, the top man always consulted his personal assistant on any major decision he took; she happened to be his mistress of some years standing and virtually ran the company.

Finding out where influence resides within a company is not always easy. Managers are often reluctant to gossip about 'influence power', especially if they themselves are victims of it. Being over-called by individuals carrying greater influence is something many managers find difficult to talk about with external salesmen. The most effective technique for finding out where these relationships exist is probably to invite an ally or coach within the client organization to construct a power map. (Power maps are described in detail in Chapter 6.)

Control of strategic resources

Some functions within organizations carry more power than others. In some insurance companies, the actuarial function is all-powerful. Aerospace companies often have a strong research and development bias, whereas the supermarket giants place emphasis on the capability of their buyers. The organization chart will indicate where different types of power reside: for example, the financial director will have a major influence over the financial resources of the organization, but may also be influential in other fields, such as business planning and forecasting. The powerful functions within the organization will be determined both by the organizational structure and by the nature of the industry in which the firm operates.

In some situations, the relative power of some functions may be dramatically changed by the sale going ahead. For instance, the information technology director may see the outsourcing of his empire as a threat to his own position, and an undermining of his own past performance. It is rare for an IT director with such perceptions to greet with enthusiasm any bid to rationalize, streamline or sort out his legacy. The salesman may need to give considerable thought to handling such a situation.

Nevertheless, in any sales campaign to outsource a major function, it is likely that the manager who heads up that function will be heavily involved in the choice of a supplier to carry out the work.

The salesman needs to consider carefully what power shifts his proposals may cause in the client organization. This should act as a guide to who might champion his proposals and who might oppose them. Calls on individual managers within the client company will need to take account of these shifts. He may need to be guided by the 'winners' in such proposals, in order to minimize opposition from the powerful quarters who may 'lose out'.

Knowledge/skills

An individual can derive power from his specialist knowledge or skills. The investment banks pay small fortunes to successful investment fund managers. Football managers pay transfer fees running into many millions to get the players they want. Some consultancies have grown into large corporations through offering specialized knowledge capital.

In a large procurement, some evaluations may be carried out by individuals with significant knowledge or skill power. Experts may be assigned to evaluating the technical and commercial ramifications of the supplier's proposition. Depending on the type of organization, the power and influence of such experts may be out of all proportion to their position in the hierarchy, or to the resources that they control. Bodies of technical competence within some client companies, particularly large bureaucracies, hold great sway in deciding which solution is best suited to the client. To sell effectively to such a company, the salesman may need to line up experts with similar technical competence and encourage relationship-building with personnel at relatively low levels within the buying organization. There may be similar cliques making legal, financial and commercial evaluations of the seller's proposition, where confidences will need to be built if the client's opinions are to be influenced.

Control of the environment

The fortunes of all companies are dictated by the external environment in which they operate. Those parties that best understand that environment can use it as a source of power within the organization. For instance, sales or marketing managers are often seen as being in touch with the external environment and are therefore more dominant in policy determination than, say, production managers.

One good question for any salesman to ask himself when trying to build the power profile of an organization is, 'Who, within the client company, are my real customers?'

If the seller's proposal endeavours to improve the sales performance of a company, then the sales director and his team are likely to be highly influential in any decision that company makes. If, on the other hand, the seller aims to cut costs and lay off staff, the finance director may be its prime customer, whilst the human resources director may wish to be closely involved in understanding and approving any plans. It is important to remember that the function initiating the request for proposal may not be the real customer. A purchasing department or an IT department may often make the request for a bid that involves a broader group of customers within the client organization. Getting to the real customers is likely to be essential if the seller's proposals are to be carried.

Exercising discretion

Johnson and Scholes define 'exercising discretion' as the final source of power. This relates to the way in which managers interpret decisions taken by their seniors, and usually resides within the middle management of an organization. A firm's top management may be involved in the major decisions, but underpinning those are hundreds and hundreds of lesser decisions that all contribute to the overall decision-making process. The middle management might exercise discretion, for example, by adjusting the respective weightings attributed to different aspects of a technical recommendation. By selective tuning of the weightings, the middle management may be able to recommend either supplier A or supplier B – in both cases they would be able to state categorically to their top management that a clear winner has been selected using the most rigorous of technical criteria.

This type of middle-management activity is prevalent in many government procurements, where public accountability means that bureaucratic rationales are often generated in order to justify major decisions. When selling to governments, working with the manager who exercises discretion in defining the decision-making grids and processes can be critical in securing a successful sale.

DECISION-MAKING PROCESSES

Fundamental to the timing and execution of any sales activity is an understanding of the client organization's decision-making process; that is, who will be making decisions, and when.

Every organization reaches its decisions in a different way. Henry Mintzberg, in his seminal work *The Structuring of Organizations*, suggests that there are six organizational configurations. His view is that decision-making characteristics are different, depending on the organizational configuration. A study of Mintzberg's theory can help the salesman to conclude how he should adapt his selling behaviour to different organizational structures. However, before we can understand Mintzberg's theory, some of his terminology requires explanation.

He defines centralization as 'keeping all the power in one place'. He distinguishes vertical decentralization – the delegation of formal power down the hierarchy to line managers – from horizontal decentralization – the extent to which formal or informal power is dispersed out of the line hierarchy to non-managers (operators, analysts and support staffers).

Mintzberg's six organizational configurations, and what he predicts for decision-making characteristics within each one, are as follows.

MINTZBERG'S ORGANIZATIONAL CONFIGURATIONS

SIMPLE STRUCTURE

MACHINE BUREAUCRACY

PROFESSIONAL BUREAUCRACY

DIVISIONALIZED FORM

ADHOCRACY

MISSIONARY

Simple structure

The simple centralized organizational structure is not much more than one unit consisting of one or a few top managers, and a group of operators to do the work. Little of the behaviour in the organization is formalized. The organization is flexible, young, entrepreneurial and needs to be dynamic in order to outsmart bureaucracies. Most small and many medium-sized firms are simple configurations.

Decisions in a simple configuration will be made by the person at the top. He may take some advice from others, but is unlikely to be unduly influenced by them, trusting more to his own intuition and judgement. With such an organization, selling to, and winning over, this person is the only activity the salesman need worry about.

Machine bureaucracy

The machine bureaucracy, born of the Industrial Revolution, with highly specialized jobs and standardized work, has an elaborate administration, comprising what Mintzberg terms a 'technostructure to design and maintain its systems of standardization'. Because the organization depends heavily on this technostructure, some decision-making power resides within it, giving rise to limited horizontal decentralization. Machine bureaucracies fit most naturally with mass production, with the majority of the staff being machine operators. Firms such as Chrysler, Hoover and Sony closely fit this definition.

Decisions in a machine bureaucracy will usually follow a well-defined process, through committees, sub-committees and expert opinions. Significant decision-making power will be bestowed on these committees, especially on the functional managers leading them. Decisions will probably be documented and passed from committee to committee, providing a decision audit trail.

The decision process in a machine bureaucracy may be confidential, but it will exist. The salesman needs to discover all that he can about the decision-making process created specifically for the situation that he is contesting. He should aim to influence and win the recommendation at each committee stage. In this type of configuration, the senior management will be influenced by the decision-making process, although it will still be possible for the salesman with strong top-management relationships to get decisions overturned at a higher level. As the middle management is organized on functional lines, a presentation to the top management that stresses cross-functional considerations can move the debate onto a different playing field, possibly not considered by any of the individual committees. The evaluation of business risk, covering such topics as the vendor's credit rating, financial stability and capability to work with the client, is often overlooked by such organizations.

Professional bureaucracy

The professional bureaucracy relies upon the standardization of skills rather than on work processes for its co-ordination. Professionals are very powerful in this environment, and have considerable control over their own work and work patterns. Mintzberg cites hospitals and universities as typical of professional bureaucracies. In fact, many government facilities are professional bureaucracies, and, as in the machine bureaucracy, decision-making will follow highly formalized processes. In the professional bureaucracy, however, much more power will reside with the professional work-force, or, in Mintzberg's terminology, there will be a high level of horizontal decentralization.

The salesman will probably need to win the intellectual argument at the working level in this type of organization; the top management will tend simply to rubber-stamp many of the committee-led decisions taken lower down. Running escalations to top managers (or, in the case of government, senior politicians) to get decisions reversed are high risk, with a low chance of success, and should only be tried as a last resort. Salesmen are likely to need assistance from technical, legal and commercial experts to win business in this sort of environment, as the client's professionals will often want to discuss every aspect of the vendor's proposal in great detail.

Some organizations choose not to sell to this type of organization as part of their portfolio planning. Selling tends to be time-consuming, overly bureaucratic and expensive. Often the buying concern insists upon penal contractual terms, focusing on getting financial recompense in the event of failure rather than on optimizing the chances of a successful implementation. The outcome of a competitive procurement may not be commercially based, as decisions tend to be taken by non-business people, such as academics, scientists and civil servants

Divisionalized form

The divisionalized form is a set of independent entities coupled together by a loose administrative structure. This type of organizational configuration is most prevalent in highly diversified organizations, where there is little synergy between the different divisions. Usually, such organizations are mature, and have run out of opportunities in their traditional markets. Divisionalization allows for functionally organized units to be restructured into market-based units, with considerable autonomy and decentralization passed down the chain of command; in Mintzberg's terms this is vertical decentralization.

Each division will have its own functional staffs, for example financial, administrative, legal and sales. Control is exerted from a small headquarters and based on performance. Often, divisions will strive to assert their independence; for example, if one buys its IT equipment from IBM, another division may buy anything but IBM. As long as the units deliver their numbers, they tend to be left alone, and allowed the autonomy to chase their chosen market opportunities. Only when performance wanes does 'help from headquarters' appear. Firms that are strongly divisionalized include BAT and Hanson.

Selling to such organizations will need to be directed towards the relevant division. Typically, each division will make its own decision on capital spending, even if a nod from HQ is required. If HQ authority is required, it will expect to have the case presented to it by the divisional management, not by the vendor. In some circumstances, the vendor may be invited to participate in the presentations by the divisional management, but unsolicited calling on the HQ management may be seen by the client as interfering and unhelpful. Decision-making at the divisional level is likely to be commercially focused, with a keen eye on the bottom line.

Adhocracy

Adhocracies are organically structured organizations that need to innovate in order to function and grow. Consulting firms, such as Booz Allen, McKinsey or Cap Gemini, are often run along these lines. A bureaucratic configuration is too inflexible and restrictive, and the simple configuration is too autocratic. These organizations need project structures, whereby experts from different specialities can be brought together into smoothly functioning creative teams. Typically, experts are grouped by speciality or competence for pay and ration purposes, but are deployed into market-based teams to do useful work. Each team, frequently based at its client's location, has a high degree of delegated decision-making power. Larger decisions will usually need to be referred to a central management team, and this can lead to such decisions being 'salami-sliced' into smaller decisions, to allow them to be taken at the project level. Power in these organizations is based on expertise and little distinction is made between line and staff functions. Emphasis is placed on co-operation between experts.

Selling to this type of organization is usually based on the vendor's competency or ability to do the job. Sellers are often selling a niche service to complement the adhocracy's capabilities in specific areas. The technical sale is usually the predominant issue, with quality, track record and ability to do the work being the key issues. Sellers need to be experts in their own right, or be prepared to allow the technicians to play a high-profile role in the selling effort. The sales effort will typically be directed towards the project head. Within an adhocracy, only a limited number of project leaders will need to spend many millions of pounds buying in expertise.

Missionary

Although the missionary configuration, Mintzberg's sixth and final configuration, does not concern the corporate salesman, it is described here with a view to completeness.

Missionary organizations are pulled together by zeal for a cause, and tend to have little formal structure or status. Examples of missionary organizations are protest groups, such as Greenpeace, charitable trusts or religious sects. By the time such an organization is big enough to make

---

**GLOBAL LIFE INSURANCE AND INTERNATIONAL CONSULTING
- CONFIGURATIONS -**

International Consulting is a typical adhocracy, with experts grouped by competence, and teams being formed as needed to address client's requirements.

The Global Life Insurance Company is predominantly a machine bureaucracy, with teams of clerical and administrative staff handling the large amounts of paperwork generated by insurance contracts.

Selling to Global Life needs to be focused on the top management and the committees formed to evaluate different aspects of the vendor's proposals. The decision-making process is likely to be bureaucratic.

---

multi-million dollar procurements (for example, the Catholic Church), it will already have acquired the characteristics of another configuration, to provide the structure and control necessary for it to function. For this reason, the missionary configuration is never encountered by a salesman selling a major deal; such activity requires financial and business controls and some kind of structure, and a missionary configuration does not have these.

SUMMARY

The way in which decision-making is distributed throughout each type of organizational configuration, and the way that influences where the seller should focus most of his sales effort is summarized on page 35.

Models exist, therefore, for ascertaining where power lies within an organization, and how decisions are made. The models can only act as a guide, because every organization is as different as the people in them. However, understanding the power relationships in the buying organization is critical to making a successful sale. Ultimately, the salesman will need to take a view on where to focus his own and his organization's own efforts. Such decisions should be taken in the light of the models described, in conjunction with any available advice from the client. Questioning the client as to how decisions will be made, by whom and when, is important intelligence that will allow the salesman and his company to focus and direct their campaign to optimum effect.

MINTZBERG'S ORGANIZATIONAL CONFIGURATIONS

WHERE DECISION-MAKING POWER LIES, AND SELLING IMPLICATIONS

Simple structure	Centralized	Sell to man at the top
Machine bureaucracy	Limited horizontal decentralization	Sell to committees and top management. Selling will be expensive and processes may be bureaucratic
Professional bureaucracy	Horizontal decentralization	Sell to committees. The technical sale is important. Top management may be a rubber-stamp with limited influence
Divisional form	Limited vertical decentralization	Sell to divisional management
Adhocracy	Selective decentralization	Sell to project leaders
Missionary	Decentralization	Not applicable

KEY POINTS

■ Understand the type of organization you are selling to, and where the power lies.

■ Understand how the organization makes its decisions.

■ Understand who will be involved in the procurement decision we are consulting.

■ Understand the source of these individuals' power.

3

CLIENT RELATIONSHIPS

I dislike arguments of any kind. They are always vulgar, and often convincing.
The Importance of Being Earnest
Oscar Wilde (1856–1900), poet and dramatist

INTRODUCTION

A public-sector organization had invited several firms to bid for the designing, building and operation of a major computer system. One consortium was the cheapest, won the technical evaluation, and the risk evaluation. The solution was the best in virtually every respect. And yet they lost the business. Why?

It was the most fundamental reason of all – relationships, or, more precisely, a lack of them. The key decision-makers did not like the staff of that particular supplier. They were arrogant. They told the client company when they were wrong, which was, unfortunately, much of the time. They delighted in pointing out how things could be done better. They revelled in their 'superiority'. They were scornful of their major competitor – a world-class systems integrator. Relationships with the client were somewhere between poor and non-existent. In the end, this was the overriding factor in the decision-making.

Having rejected the bid of that consortium, the client relished explaining precisely why. From the most senior government officials down, all the people in the client organization agreed that its services were no longer required.

It was a devastating lesson for the selling company. It led them to reappraise their sales and marketing methods, personnel selection and sales training. Within a year, the firm had restructured its selling. Relationship-building skills became the most important personal characteristic required of staff wishing to progress to the higher echelons of management. Many years later, the firm is wiser as a result of its experience and is presently enjoying much greater sales success.

What the firm had failed to comprehend was the most fundamental lesson of all – that people buy from people they like and trust.

Usually, the bigger the contract, the bigger the risks, and the more important the relationship, therefore. That relationship has to be one of mutual trust, reflecting a shared commitment to see the programme through to a successful conclusion. Any client spending millions of dollars on a high-profile, high-risk project will want to be assured that when things start to go wrong, the vendor will be there sorting out the problems rather than apportioning blame.

BALANCE IN THE RELATIONSHIP

What do we mean by a 'relationship'?

Much depends upon the context. The definition will vary whether we are talking about relations, friends or business acquaintances. It can describe the sharing of a real blood-line, or a legal linkage. It can refer to a cohabiting couple, to a strong personal attraction, or to people who simply know each other. At its most fundamental, the term describes a situation where two people are eliciting a response from each other.

Within a business context, there are usually two aspects to a relationship that interest us – business and personal. A strong business relationship exists when both parties, as a result of their professional behaviour, cooperate in order to further each other's perceived business interests.

A strong business relationship exists more readily if there is a strong personal relationship. A good personal relationship helps to promote better understanding and more effective communication. This can be enhanced by engaging in social activity – for example, a drink together, a round of golf, or a trip to a Grand Prix – outside the business environment. Recognition of the benefits of good personal relationships has led to the recent boom in corporate entertaining, with business partners being treated to events as diverse as the Superbowl, the Chelsea Flower Show and Grand Opera in Venice. Incidentally, that boom has led to a dramatic rise in ticket prices for many events, and corporate entertaining has often attracted adverse publicity for putting those events beyond the means of real enthusiasts.

Salesmen wishing to develop effective relationships need to be aware of the balance between the personal and the business. If there is too strong a bias towards a personal friendship, it can be awkward to raise difficult issues. If there is too little bias, confronting sensitive personal issues may be equally awkward.

When I was a young salesman, many years ago, I knew a senior director for a major client who liked to play cards each Friday lunch-time. I thought that being invited to join his card school was an honour, and assumed it would lead to a stronger business relationship. Once I had accepted an invitation to play on a regular basis with him, we quickly became good friends. However, we rarely talked about work, despite my best efforts. As time went on, it became increasingly difficult to raise any topic related to business. During card games, he would dismiss all my attempts to steer the conversation towards work with a dismissive 'I don't want to talk about that here – what's your bid?' Each time I called his office to fix up a meeting, his secretary would say, 'He can't talk now. He says ask him about it when you meet next Friday.' When I did manage to set up formal meetings in his office, he would always want to talk about the other card players in the school. He was embarrassed about being seen to favour a friend and I was sensitive to being accused of capitalizing on a friendship. I had got the balance wrong between my personal and business relationship.

When the balance is wrong, the salesman may find it difficult to raise important business or personal issues that need resolution during a sales campaign (*see* Figure 3.1). With the right balance, a mutually beneficial environment of confidence and trust can be generated, where real issues can be sensibly and rationally debated and resolved in a satisfactory way.

Much relationship-building revolves around respect and interest. If you show someone respect, by listening attentively to what they have to

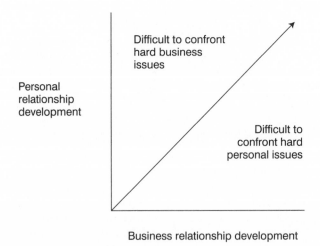

Figure 3.1: *Getting the relationship balance right*

say, that person will, in turn, be more inclined to listen to you. Respect is usually mutual. If you are dismissive or show a lack of interest, the odds are that you will not gain the other person's respect. If you show a genuine interest, they will usually reciprocate.

The objective of relationship-building is to build trust. Once a high degree of trust has been established, sensitive business issues can be addressed and resolved effectively, to the mutual benefit of both parties. Trust is, however, a fragile flower, easily damaged in stormy weather, and often killed completely by a single thoughtless act. Once destroyed, it may never be re-created, despite all efforts to bring it back to life.

Some relationships become so strong that the individual switches sides, or 'goes local'. Sales management must always be on the look-out for the salesman who stops representing his own company's best interests, and starts making unreasonable demands on his company in order to meet the needs of the customer. These can vary, from meeting impossible delivery schedules to selling at unacceptably low profit margins; from signing up to impossibly high damages terms to promising the provision of large amounts of free technical support. The salesman who 'goes local' is a major problem for a selling organization. The client company will usually see such an individual as its champion and may manipulate the selling organization in order to retain that salesperson *in situ*.

COACHES AND ENEMIES

The client taking the vendor's side in a sales campaign can be the answer to a salesman's prayer. Such individuals are usually referred to as 'coaches'. Every successful selling organization should actively look for coaches in the client organization, as these people will guide and steer the vendor's sales effort from the inside.

What motivates a coach to help a particular vendor can vary. The most positive reason is that he believes that the supplier's solution is the best for his company. He sees it as his duty to ensure that the 'right' bid wins, and therefore goes out of his way to help the bidder. Coaches may also side with a supplier through a simple desire to be helpful, because of a good relationship with that company, because he dislikes a competitor or in the pursuit of personal gain.

Broadly, there are three types of coach, differentiated by the degree to which they are able to help the salesman and by what they stand to gain from the outcome of the decision-making process.

Native guide

This type of coach understands the workings of the customer's organization. He explains the politics and power bases within the firm and why previous decisions were taken. He may not be involved in the sales decision at all.

I would always attempt to find two or three native guides to give me an insight into the people and politics of the firm to which I was selling. Reliance on just one risks exposure to personal bias.

Once selected, it is usually straightforward to approach native guide coaches. Many are flattered to be asked about their own organization and most feel that it is something they are well qualified to discuss.

Adviser-teacher

Adviser-teachers coach the salesman on progress, and advise and direct him. They can be outside, but are usually inside the client organization.

The adviser-teacher often initiates contact with the salesman, by offering information. By developing the relationship, the salesman may convert this one-off action into an on-going supply of valuable intelligence. Adviser-teachers will also tell the salesman where he is going wrong, and what he needs to do to correct his problems. They can therefore often seem negative and unhelpful. It is important, however, that such criticism is not interpreted by salesmen as a sign of rejection; in most cases, it is the opposite.

An adviser-teacher coach provides negative feedback, which allows the salesman to correct his performance. Feedback should be actively encouraged and solicited once offered. The coach should be made aware of the value of his advice. He will be all the more willing to offer advice next time if rewarded by gratitude, whatever personal offence the advice might have caused.

Friend

Friends are the most powerful type of coach. Friends win when the salesman wins, and lose when the salesman loses. Friends fight for the salesman's solution.

If friends have been into a meeting and have fired off all of the positive messages about the vendor's solution, they will often come back for more information in specific areas, especially when an outright win has not been secured. Again, the coach may exhibit signs of frustration or annoyance whilst undertaking this activity. This may be because he is under stress, and has failed to achieve all the situation offered. It is important not to interpret such behaviour as negative towards the vendor or his solution, and to provide as much help as possible. A strong partnership with an effective coach will often be candid and painful, but ultimately highly productive and rewarding.

All types of coach can provide salespeople with invaluable information from which to build a successful sales campaign. They may let the salesman know who his friends and enemies are, when key meetings will take place, who holds the real decision-making power, and how decisions are made. Coaches provide intelligence that allows the salesman to fine-tune and direct his sales efforts to the maximum advantage. They can pinpoint the key actions that are needed if the doubters in the client company are to be won over and advise on how to capitalize on competitors' weaknesses. A good coach is worth any number of executive calls, demonstrations or site visits. If a salesman is to maximize his chances of winning, the search for a coach is of paramount importance.

Enemies

The client who is uncritical, who never provides negative feedback, and who always says everything is fine should be handled very carefully. Such people may be 'enemies', keen not to help the sales effort by providing useful advice. Coaches can help the salesman spot such individuals, but he can often spot them too. First, he should watch out for soothing generalities and platitudes, with little real information; for key questions being ducked or evaded; he should be wary of extreme civility, with little tangible evidence of a desire to develop a real understanding or appreciation of the sales proposition. These are all classical behaviours exhibited by enemies. The salesman should also look out for negative body language, such as a failure to make eye contact at critical moments, or a tense manner.

In almost every competitive sales campaign, there will be some enemies in the client organization. The successful salesman needs to find out who they are, and devise strategies either to win them over or to reduce their influence.

ESTABLISHING A RELATIONSHIP

Perhaps the most important factor to bear in mind at all times is that client personnel are first and foremost human beings. It is a mistake to assume that they will be interested only in the sales proposal, and nothing else. They may have other issues that they want to talk about, because those issues are pre-eminent on their agenda.

On one occasion I visited an IT manager to discuss supplying him with some workstations. He seemed disinterested in what I was saying, and it was clear that his mind was not on me or on our meeting. As we talked, his telephone rang, and he snatched at it. In fact, it was only his secretary with a relatively unimportant message, but he was obviously on edge and more tense than usual. I stopped trying to talk about business and asked him what was uppermost in his mind at present. He apologized: 'Actually, I am a little distracted. My daughter has just gone into hospital today, expecting her first baby.' I suddenly remembered that, some months ago, he had mentioned his daughter's pregnancy to me, and had told me that there had been some complications. Now that she had gone into hospital, he was very concerned. I kicked myself for having forgotten about the pregnancy, and vowed to make better notes about my clients in future. Remembering important personal events can be a strong relationship-builder, and can be used to great effect in breaking the ice at the start of a subsequent meeting.

Realizing that my client was not going to give his full attention to my workstation proposals on this occasion, I apologized for my insensitivity and suggested that we re-schedule the meeting for a week's time. He was only too pleased to agree. We then talked for half an hour about the worries of parenthood, how one never stops being concerned about one's own children, and how excited he was about the imminent arrival of his first grandchild. One week later, we met in a nearby restaurant to celebrate a trouble-free birth and to discuss my workstation proposal: I had his complete attention and, after an hour's discussion, had closed the order.

Of course, not every meeting will be interrupted by quite such a dramatic personal event, but there is an important principle – be sensitive to the person on the other side of the desk, who is a human being, with a variety of emotions and aspirations. His concerns may not always be the same as yours. He may well have different interests, different priorities and different needs. The good salesman attempts to understand what these are, and to relate to them.

FACTORS IN BUILDING A BUSINESS RELATIONSHIP

The most important factor to bear in mind when building a relationship is the client's interest. By trying to see the world through the client's eyes, the salesman is more likely to gain his attention and to understand his motives and actions.

In planning to talk to individuals within the client organization, I always focus on the following three broad areas:

❑ the individual's buyer values;
❑ the individual's level in the organization;
❑ the behaviour that is most appropriate to that individual, depending on his personality type.

Attention to these three areas when planning a visit to a client can be useful in helping the salesman to see the world through the client's eyes.

Buyer values

When I run sales-awareness workshops for managers, I often start by asking participants to think of something they have bought recently, from a new car to a tube of toothpaste. I then ask them to list the two or three key reasons why they bought their item. It is always a revealing exercise for them, and for me, as it continually underlines the diversity of the reasons why people buy products. Below is a list of some of the more common buyer values, recorded over the many times I have played the game. (Some of the less common but more esoteric ones have been omitted – one attractive young woman said she had bought a new BMW because she thought it was 'sexy'; a middle-aged bachelor bought a new bed in an attempt to entice his new girlfriend into it.)

Clients typically have two types of buyer value: personal and business. Personal buyer values are those that relate to people acting for their own benefit, while business buyer values relate to them acting for the benefit of their business. The list shows business buyer values, which relate to the product or service being purchased. On page 43 is a list of some typical personal buyer values.

SOME COMMON BUYER VALUES

GOOD PRICE	GOOD DEAL
VALUE FOR MONEY	FREE GIFT
QUALITY	UNIQUE SOLUTION
SPECIAL PROMOTION	ENVIRONMENTAL RECORD
GOOD PRODUCT	AVAILABILITY OF PRODUCT
FREE DELIVERY OFFER	NICE COLOUR
DISLIKE OF A COMPETITIVE PRODUCT	GOOD ADVERTISEMENT
VENDOR'S REPUTATION	FREE GUARANTEE
RECOMMENDATION OF A FRIEND	LOCATION OF SHOP

SOME PERSONAL BUYER VALUES

A MORE INTERESTING JOB

A BETTER-PAID JOB

A LESS STRESSFUL JOB

MORE RESPONSIBILITY

MORE TIME AT HOME

THE OPPORTUNITY TO BUILD AN EMPIRE

THE OPPORTUNITY TO TRAVEL ABROAD

MORE POWER

MORE JOB SECURITY

In some instances, the buyer value will appeal to both personal and business interests, and this type of value is particularly effective in a sales campaign. An example of how both can be addressed simultaneously to powerful effect is illustrated by the real-life case study on page 45.

Everyone makes purchases for a multitude of different reasons, and not all the reasons are logical or declared up-front. Few people would admit to buying something because they liked the salesman or because they liked the packet. Yet, in selling, these are precisely two reasons that decide winners and losers. Why else would corporations spend so much money on training their sales-force or packaging their produce? Finding out, interpreting and understanding the client's buyer values – what will make them buy – is fundamental to successful selling.

Once the salesman has understood a client's buyer values, it is up to him to rationalize why his solution best addresses them. Arguments that are made in the buyer's language and that offer benefits that can be related to those values, are more likely to find resonance with the buyer than lists of product features. Modifying a solution to address a key individual's buyer values is often necessary to conclude a sale.

Level in organizations

People at different levels in an organization have different types of responsibility.

A CEO or chairman should be taking a cross-company view of any decision and should be considering long-term strategy. A middle

---

LINKING PERSONAL AND BUSINESS BUYER VALUES

The Regal Investment Bank had decided to outsource its IT department, and to contract to hire back its computer service from the successful bidder for the next seven years. The Regal Investment Bank was in need of cash, and had decided that IT was not a core competence. Selling off the IT department, and hiring back their computer services, seemed a sensible business approach. The IT director, who was due to retire in six months, was put in charge of selecting a company to perform the outsourcing.

Several vendor companies bid packages that were broadly similar in total financial value to Regal Investment. However, one firm, International Consulting, discovered how the key buyer, the IT director, would be compensated for successfully outsourcing his IT department. It transpired that he was to be financially rewarded by bonus based on an algorithm heavily weighted by the cash value that the successful outsourcing company placed on the assets to be outsourced, the hardware, software, people and other resources that comprised the IT department. The reason for this bonus was that the IT director had been responsible for building up the department over several years, and the selling company wanted to reward him for those efforts as part of a generous 'golden handshake'.

International Consulting accordingly made some adjustments to their bid. They artificially inflated the value of the IT asset by 40 per cent. They calculated that this additional cash outlay could be recovered over the period of the contract by:

❏ extending the period of the contract from seven to ten years and

❏ accelerating their planned cost reduction programme.

No change was made to the annual cost of the outsourcing contract to Regal Investment, so that the price of providing the service during the first seven years looked as competitive as before.

In altering the shape of the deal in this way, both business and personal buyer values were improved. Regal Investment got a larger up-front cash payment, and the IT director received a more generous bonus. The only apparent downside was that the Regal Investment Bank was required to commit to extending their contract period from seven to ten years, a small price to pay against the strong upsides on offer. International Consulting won the business.

(*The names of the companies in this true case study have been changed.*)

manager will probably be taking a more functional view that embraces both strategic and operational considerations. A technician will usually perform operational tasks – perspective and judgement will be conditioned by the narrower framework within which he operates. In selling to any large organization, it is important to bear in mind the level of the individual, and to pitch messages accordingly.

Getting to the person at the top of an organization is very important, as he can be asked ultimately to overrule or influence decision-making anywhere within the organization. If the salesman thinks himself into that person's mind-set, and takes a strategic view of the issue he wishes to influence, he may be able to create a series of arguments that builds a decision in his favour.

Consider the following example: A technical evaluator lower down in the organization may have decided that a competitor has a better technical solution to his company's requirement, having looked at the need and at the competitor's technical capabilities. It would be ideal to get this decision reversed at the technical level, either by introducing other technical factors, or by enhancing the technical strength of the bid. However, this may not be possible. If the supplier has lost the decision because of a technical recommendation, that supplier's salesman may still be able to win the sale by introducing other, broader factors at a more senior level. The fact that the competitor has a lower credit rating, or has never handled a bid of such a size before, may make it possible for the salesman to build a case to win over the CEO. He may prefer to accept the bid which, although its solution may not quite meet all of the technical requirements, comes from a lower-risk organization with which to do business.

It is important to recognize that both the technical and the strategic perspectives are valid within an organization, although they may give different answers. In order to sell successfully, it is important to understand which parties the solution is likely to appeal to most, and ensure that the evaluation gives due weight to them. In building a sales message for individual calls on particular decision-makers, it is critically important to take account of the organizational level of the evaluators, and the terms of reference to which they are working in making their evaluations.

Behaviour and personality type

There are many different personality types within every organization. Differences in psychological make-up cause people to think in different ways, react to pressure differently, and ask for different types of information before making decisions. By observing and understanding the way in which people react, it is possible for the salesman to adapt his behaviour in order to sell more effectively. This is the third critical factor in building relationships.

This area of behavioural science has been enthusiastically embraced by consultants in recent years, and now forms the basis of many sales and management training courses. It is an important area for the corporate salesman, and Chapter 4 is devoted to it.

KEY POINTS

■ Strike the right balance between the business and the personal relationship.

■ Identify friends and enemies.

■ Find and develop coaches – they will be invaluable in guiding our campaign.

■ Show respect to the client – it is usually mutual.

■ Relate to the client's interests – see the world through the client's eyes.

4

SELLING BEHAVIOUR

To be natural is such a very difficult pose to keep up.

An Ideal Husband

Oscar Wilde (1856–1900), poet and dramatist

INTRODUCTION

When a client contracts for a complex deal, what is he buying from the vendor?

It is usually more than just a product. Even deals with a major product component need support services.

By some definitions, a complex deal embraces the provision of new ideas, technologies, skills and processes, woven together by detailed contractual agreements. However, to characterize deals in this way is to risk understating the totality of what a buyer seeks from the solution-provider.

In my experience, what a client wants most of all is a relationship of trust and understanding with the solution-provider. Most clients have an over-riding need for a business partner who understands them, who is sensitive to their needs, and who will be there when things go wrong. The client's wants and needs are seldom articulated in this way, however, and with good reason – clients have their pride, and a measure of distance and impartiality has to be maintained during the proposal process.

The reason why clients seek this kind of relationship with suppliers has much to do with the nature of complex bids. The most sophisticated buyer can get only an impression of what any supplier can offer, however rigorous and detailed the procurement process. Any major decision will therefore contain an element of 'gut feeling', and this relies as much on the relationship between the buying and selling organizations as on the technical merits of the proposed solution. Many managers and professionals trained to offer technical solutions may not have very good relationship-building skills. However, by considering and using a few simple models, everyone is able to modify their behaviour and enhance their capability for building relationships.

At the root of the models discussed later in this chapter lies one principle: the better the salesman understands his client, the better equipped he will be to adapt his behaviour in order to communicate more effectively. Through understanding what motivates and drives the client, the supplier can offer propositions and ideas in terms that will be more appealing and acceptable than a bland statement of capability . This section concentrates on a few of the better-known behavioural models, and applies them directly to the practical business of selling. I have found each of the models described to be of great value throughout my professional life. They offer a powerful framework within which to consider the behaviour of others, as well as providing a mirror for self-reflection.

MOTIVATION

Why is it that people climb mountains and swim rivers? Why do explorers explore and philosophers philosophize? Why do we race and fight one another in sports events, and in life? Why do we spend years and years working, often for the financial gain of others? Why do we fall in love? What is it that motivates us to do the things we do?

Charles Handy, in the context of considering the motivation to work, asserts that there is 'no guaranteed formula of motivation' (Handy, 1993). However, he claims that 'there is now a much better understanding of the process by which an individual reaches decisions on the apportionment of his or her ambitions, time, energy and talent'. He goes on to outline three types of early motivation theory:

❏ satisfaction theories;
❏ incentive theories;
❏ intrinsic theories.

Each of these can be applied to corporate selling.

Satisfaction theories

This group of theories attempts to correlate a worker's state of satisfaction with performance. Perhaps the best-known contributor to this category of theory is Fred Herzberg.

Herzberg was a behavioural scientist who published his pioneering work on motivation in the 1950s and 1960s. He is best known for his two-factor theory, the basis of which is that it is possible to distinguish between factors that satisfy and factors that dissatisfy. Herzberg referred to the factors that satisfy as 'motivators'; those that dissatisfy are 'hygiene factors'. The most interesting aspect of his work is the discovery that dealing with the dissatisfying factors does not produce satisfaction; it merely prevents dissatisfaction.

Whilst Herzberg's theory was most commonly applied to motivation in the workplace, his work can also stimulate us to think what might cause a client to become satisfied or dissatisfied with a sales proposition. For instance, if a proposal is truly to inspire a client, it must *motivate* him. In my experience, propositions that display creativity, flair, innovation and excitement are powerful client motivators. Value propositions can also be strong motivators. A proposition that displays such qualities has a good chance of capturing the client's imagination, and this will work powerfully in the vendor's favour when the evaluations are made.

The second, equally important aspect of Herzberg's work relates to dissatisfiers, or hygiene factors. Herzberg concluded that, if these were not right, all the satisfying in the world would not prevent dissatisfaction. In my experience of making sales propositions, elements that cause dissatisfaction, if they do not meet certain minimum requirements, include the technical viability of the solution, the business risk inherent in the solution, and the contractual terms applicable to the deal. These can all be hygiene factors. If the bond of trust between the salesman and the client has been broken, it can cause the client significant dissatisfaction.

Herzberg's view is that, however motivating a proposition may be, it is unlikely to be effective in preventing dissatisfaction if the hygiene factors are not right. Of course, generating some client dissatisfaction does not necessarily mean that the proposition will fail. The lesson to take from Herzberg is that the supplier needs to think carefully about which factors are likely to motivate the client and then to test whether or not these generate any adverse hygiene factor, such as a different contractual condition. At that point, careful soundings need to be taken from the client, and advice sought, before we propose such motivators. For example,

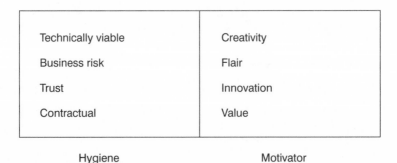

Technically viable	Creativity
Business risk	Flair
Trust	Innovation
Contractual	Value

Hygiene   Motivator

Figure 4.1: *Motivators and hygiene factors based on Herzberg's two-factor theory*

over-engineering a solution, however technically attractive and creative this may be, could generate a significant hygiene factor, such as increased risk, that could increase client dissatisfaction.

In many situations, the most important factor for a salesman to consider in the context of satisfiers and dissatisfiers is the *price* of his proposition. He should endeavour to understand whether a good price is a positive motivator, or a bad price is a hygiene factor, or dissatisfier. Depending on the situation, price can fall into either category. For example, in many UK public-sector procurements, a low price is a motivator. As long as all other factors are satisfactory, the lowest price will often win the business. However, in many private-sector bids, as long as the price is not hopelessly out of line, other factors (such as perceived business value) may sway the choice of supplier; in other words, the price of the deal is more of a hygiene factor. Understanding the client's view of price can influence whether a supplier wishes to bid at all for business with the client and, if so, how to pitch the price of any proposition made. Misreading how the client will interpret price factors can cost both sides dearly; in the worst case, it can make the difference between winning and losing the contract.

Incentive theories

Incentive theories relate to the provision of a reward in order to achieve a given behaviour.

There is often a link between incentive and reward in the context of selling activity. Eurostar offers its regular customers free trips from Europe to New York or Hong Kong; American Airlines offers members of its frequent-flyer programme access to its lavish Admiral Club departure lounges; the major credit card companies offer benefits to customers making purchases with their cards. These organizations are offering a reward in an attempt to persuade customers to buy or use their product regularly; using this kind of incentive is a very common method of encouraging a consumer to buy a product or service.

The use of incentives and rewards in corporate selling is also common; so common, in fact, that it is accepted by many as part of normal business behaviour, and an integral part of the selling process. A business lunch (incentive) offered by the seller may be the mechanism for obtaining information (reward) from the client. An invitation to a concert at Carnegie Hall or Covent Garden (incentive) might open the door to a previously unreachable executive (reward). Although these are examples of fairly small incentives offered in the hope of reaping some reward, they are an accepted part of business life in the West and frequently achieve the hoped-for behaviour change. In some parts of the world, local practice may be routinely more excessive. For example, in many countries, public-sector contracts (reward) can be 'bought' by greasing the palm (incentive) of the appropriate civil servant.

The process of using any incentive/reward technique to sway a buyer to favour a proposal should be carefully weighed. Too small an incentive may not achieve the required behaviour change. Too generous an incentive runs the risk of being interpreted as a bribe, which can instantly destroy a relationship, and even a career. Guy Snowden, chairman of GTech, was accused of offering a bribe to Virgin's founder and chairman Richard Branson in 1993. In court it was alleged that Snowden had attempted to persuade Branson not to bid for the UK's national lottery. Following a court case in 1998, Snowden was found guilty. It led to his resignation from the board of Camelot, the company that won the franchise to run the lottery, and from GTech. Any salesman contemplating the use of an incentive/reward motivator should carefully sound out the client to establish that the incentive will be seen as a positive gesture, rather than as a crude attempt to 'buy his vote'.

There are many subtle variations on the type of incentive that can be offered by a selling organization. There are also many ways to relieve the buyer's conscience, by making the acceptance of such offers above board, and acceptable to external scrutiny. For example, the vendor organization may know that the buyer's key decision-maker likes foreign travel. The salesman may suggest to that person that a better evaluation of his proposal might be made by visiting some clients on the other side of the Atlantic. Here, both sides may find it more acceptable to run with the assumption that the only consideration is the business content of the visit. Some firms even insist upon paying their own expenses on such trips, believing that it makes the arrangement less compromising. My own view is that such practice has little impact on the incentive/reward equation. Any individual accepting such an invitation will inevitably feel indebted to the selling firm making the invitation, regardless of who is paying the air fare.

As a final word on incentive/reward motivators, it is perhaps worth mentioning that salesmen on commission are, themselves, participating in such a scheme. They have a financial incentive – the promise of commission payments – to sell and deliver their company's product.

Intrinsic theories

These theories relate to the belief that, as humans, we all have needs that can be satisfied by pursuing certain courses of action. Looking at buyer values (*see* Chapter 3) helps the vendor identify what a buyer wants; if the salesman addresses these needs, he can advance his own interests more effectively.

At a more general level, the humanistic psychologist Abraham Maslow concluded that people's needs or desires are only motivators when they are unsatisfied, and that these unsatisfied needs can shape a person's views and values. He proposed that people's needs follow a well-defined pattern – this is referred to as 'Maslow's hierarchy of needs' (Maslow, 1968). Only when his lower-order needs have been satisfied will a person think about the next level of needs within the hierarchy. Maslow proposed that people are more likely to be attracted by a proposition that meets their current needs, rather than one that attends to those needs that have already been met. In a selling environment, this means that the salesman should articulate his proposition in terms that meet the client's *unsatisfied* needs.

Maslow's hierarchy is shown in Figure 4.2. Needs are organized in order of importance, the most important – physiological needs – being at the base of the triangle.

Physiological needs – food, drink and shelter – are basic to human survival. No client is likely to be deprived of these needs in the long term. However, in the normal course of doing business, physiological needs can come to the fore – hunger can set in; a 'comfort break' may be necessary. At such times, the client's attention can wander, until the immediate physiological need is satisfied. A sensible salesman will ensure that presentations and meetings are structured in such a way as to ensure that the client has the opportunity to satisfy his physiological needs, before they disturb his ability to concentrate on the matter in hand.

Once physiological needs have been satisfied, the next level in the hierarchy is safety. These needs relate to an individual's desire for protection, predictability and stability. In selling to people who put a high priority on these factors, the salesman should endeavour to stress the safety of his

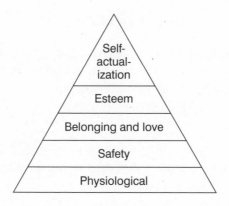

Figure 4.2: *Maslow's hierarchy of needs*

offerings, the contractual commitments his company is prepared to make, their readiness to share risk and their track record of trouble-free implementation. Reference visits should reinforce the successful way in which similar work has been implemented.

Once safety needs have been satisfied, people transfer their needs to 'belongingness and love'. Such people want to be liked, and will become offended or hurt if they sense that they are being omitted from groups or gatherings. Such individuals will value strong personal relationships with the supplier.

After belonging needs, esteem needs come to the fore. These relate to respect, status and recognition. Look out for the prominent, even ostentatious display of other 'proofs' of 'having arrived' – the Gucci handbag or the Rolex watch, for example. Having identified such people, capitalize on their need for esteem by introducing them to senior management, and by asking them to speak as 'thought leaders' or 'leading customers' at the supplier's own company meetings.

When all the subservient needs are satisfied, people turn to the highest level of desire. Self-actualization means being emotionally fulfilled as well as continuing to develop professionally and personally. Selling to these people is less prescriptive. The best approach is to discover what their real interests are, and to build on those. Self-actualizers will tend to appreciate an environment of innovation and creativity, where they have more freedom to express themselves and their ideas.

In our case study, we have decided that Simon Nutt is sympathetic to International Consulting's ideas for Global Life. The text on the following page applies both Maslow and Herzberg theories to suggest a course of action to strengthen his support for us.

PERSONALITY TYPE

It has been recognized for many centuries that people have different personalities. The ancient Greeks thought that the body contained four 'humours' – yellow bile, black bile, phlegm and blood. They believed that an individual's personality could be attributed to the mix of humours in their body. Although medical science ultimately discredited this particular theory, psychologists have continued to develop new and diverse theories of personality type and trait. Whilst individual theories differ, the following principles, which are common to most to them, are of interest to the salesman:

❑ people exhibit different personality traits;
❑ different personality types perceive information in different ways;
❑ different personality types make judgements in different ways;

MOTIVATION AND NEEDS FOR SIMON NUTT

Simon Nutt is a relatively new recruit to Global Life. He is thirty, ambitious and flamboyant. He is married, with two young daughters. He has been a friend of Albert Stead, the strategy and planning manager, for many years.

Nutt does not get on well with his manager, Mike Chadwick. Chadwick is fifty-six, and has been the IT director for six years, having come up through the ranks. He has been with Global Life for over thirty years. Nutt sees the need for change, whereas Chadwick tends to resist it. As a result, there has been tension between them over the scope of the back-office project. Recently, Chadwick has warned him to concentrate on performing his current job properly, and not to get grandiose ideas about changing the world.

In our discussions with Nutt, his major concern is the vulnerability of his position at Global Life. He understands the need for the changes that the new top management team is introducing. However, following Chadwick's warning, he is keen to ensure that any implementation for which he is responsible should be successful. In Maslow's terms, he has unsatisfied safety needs with regard to his job at Global Life. Because of this, he has been keen to stress that, whatever solution we propose, it must be viable.

However, he is excited by International Consulting's suggestions not just to reduce cost, but also to develop simultaneously a new, integrated product engine, capable of bringing new financial products to market more quickly. Financial markets around the world are changing rapidly, and a firm that is able to bring new products to market rapidly should have a strong competitive edge. Nutt sees our suggestions as delivering the vehicle to enable Global Life to become more competitive. In Herzberg's terms, this is a major motivator for Nutt in considering our proposals.

International Consulting has recently completed a project to streamline National Mutual's back office. The scope of the work performed there is similar to that we are now suggesting to Global Life, including the introduction of a new product engine. To address Nutt's safety need and to motivate him further, International Consulting's salesman, Chris Newton, has decided to take Nutt on a reference visit to National Mutual. There, he plans to demonstrate how International Consulting has successfully streamlined and enhanced National Mutual's back office. His message to Nutt will be that International Consulting has the resources and skills to develop a streamlined and sophisticated back office capable of delivering the top management's vision. In addition, he will use the visit to encourage Nutt's enthusiasm for widening the scope of the project to include the development of a new product engine.

The objective of the visit is therefore to address Nutt's safety needs, as well motivating him to support International Consulting's solution.

❑ by adapting the way in which information is presented, we can improve or impede effective communication;
❑ by adapting our own personality type, we can improve or impede relationship-building.

Personality models provide the salesman with a framework within which to think about a client's personality, and therefore can help to stimulate ways to develop and improve client relationships.

MBTI

Much early pioneering work on personality was done by Swiss psychiatrist, scholar and scientist Carl G. Jung (1875–1961). Jung was a disciple of Sigmund Freud and performed his pioneering work on personality type in the early part of the twentieth century.

Jung's work is deeply technical and difficult for the lay person to decipher. His ideas have, however, been widely adopted and developed for use in the business and academic world. One of the best-known and most widely used of personality-type models is the Myers-Briggs Type Indicator, or MBTI (Myers, 1987). The indicator can give us an insight both into our own personality and into that of others.

The MBTI reports personality preferences for the individual being assessed along four scales:

❑ Introvert (I) – Extrovert (E);
❑ Sensing (S) – Intuition (N);
❑ Thinking (T) – Feeling (F);
❑ Judging (J) – Perceiving (P).

Each of these scales is a continuum; for example, most people have a mixture of introvert and extrovert personality type in their psychological make-up, but one type is usually more dominant than the other. Myers-Briggs defines an individual's personality type by the four dominant preferences along the four scales. For example, an individual with dominant extrovert, intuitive, thinking, perceiving traits is an 'ENTP type'. Each of the sixteen possible combinations of preference defines a different personality type, each with its own strengths and weaknesses.

It is important for the salesman to think about personality type. By understanding his own personality, and the personality of his clients, he can adapt his approach to work more effectively with them. By working more effectively, the relationship is built. By building the relationship, the salesman increases his chances of sales success. Conversely, by ignoring a client's personality type, the salesman risks increasing conflict, especially when dealing with a personality very different from his own. To communicate effectively, the salesman should always try to adapt his style to that of the client.

Extroverts and introverts

This scale relates to where people focus their attention.

Extroverts tend to be outgoing, and like the company of other people. They prefer to communicate by talking, and are usually good, confident presenters. Actors are often extrovert.

Any activity, either social or business, that affords opportunities to talk together is likely to be good for building a relationship with an extrovert. Inviting an extrovert client to address an internal meeting of the supplier company could be effective. Putting extroverts together in an environment where they can spark off from each other's ideas can provide useful input to brainstorming sessions. In a social context, invitations to events with larger groups of people – an afternoon at the races, a banquet, or a convention – are worth considering as appropriate relationship-building tactics.

Extroverts selling to introverts risk being seen as shallow. When dealing with introverts, extrovert salesmen need to be sure they can justify their statements and must take care not to overstate their case. When dealing with introverts, extroverts may need to force themselves to be more formal and restrained than they would normally choose to be.

Introverts prefer their own company and are drawn to their inner world. They tend to be more private and reflect before speaking. They prefer to communicate by writing. Authors are often introverts.

Salesmen wishing to find suitable social vehicles for relationship-building with introverts might consider events such as a visit to the opera, ballet, or theatre, possibly with partners. These can provide an environment requiring little 'small talk'. The number of people attending meals out should be restricted to a minimum.

Introverts selling to extroverts risk being seen as unenthusiastic and reserved in their relationships.

Sensing and intuitive types

This scale relates to the way in which individuals take in information.

Sensing types like to see, touch and feel. They like detail and practicality, and tend to be meticulous about data and information. They can be good at work needing a high degree of precision. They are methodical, and focus on what they are given, rather than acting on inspiration or gut feeling. Accountants are often sensing types.

Selling to sensing types, the salesman needs to demonstrate things in a real and tangible way. Proposals should contain plenty of corroborating detail to back up any assertions made. Salesmen need to be able to follow through their arguments to a detailed degree. In order to reassure sensing clients that the capabilities they want are available, sales campaign tactics could include the following: making reference visits to other customer sites, creating working mock-up demonstrations of aspects of the solution, or talking to other clients to understand their own experiences.

Intuitives like to see the big picture. They will want to see that proposals have been thought through, and are consistent with long-term patterns and strategy. They like analogies and models. They will value creativity, innovative approaches, and qualities such as thought leadership. Politicians are often intuitive types.

Selling to intuitives, the salesman needs to ensure that his proposals are set within a strategic context. Many intuitives will only read the management summary of a proposal, and this should be high-level and concise if it is to retain the intuitive reader's interest. Intuitives can become impatient with too much detail.

Strongly intuitive salesmen selling to sensing types risk being seen as too free and easy, and too conceptual.

Thinking and feeling types

This scale relates to people's decision-making style.

Thinking types like analysis and logic. They base their decisions on objective evidence and facts rather than on emotion, and are able to rationalize their actions from the statistics or evidence in their possession. Thinkers can sometimes be seen as clinical, lacking in emotion, and unintentionally hurtful. They can be good at analysis of what is wrong. Management consultants are often thinking types.

Selling to thinkers, the salesman should be business-like and objective, using reasoned arguments that have been well thought through. Thinkers like information to be presented in a structured way, and will usually respond positively to cause-and-effect logic. The salesman needs to concentrate on facts, tasks and actions.

Feeling individuals make decisions based on values such as understanding, sympathy and recognition of people. They tend to dislike conflict. They will attribute weight to personal customer testimonials and to the opinions of those whom they trust. Social workers are often feeling types.

Selling to feeling types, the salesman should to try to take an interest in the client as a person. Asking about the family, holidays or hobbies as part of the preamble to a meeting will generally be appreciated.

Judging and perceiving types

This scale relates to how an individual orients towards the outside world.

Judging types like a plan and dislike having it interrupted. They tend to prepare things in advance, by producing lists, agendas, work plans and timetables, and like to work through projects in an orderly sequence. Judging types will let their opinion be known quickly and often forcibly. They will tend to behave formally and hold well-structured meetings. Referees and umpires are often judgmental types.

Selling to judging types can be exciting – they are usually comfortable making decisions with a minimal amount of information. A judging type is sometimes seen as a 'loose cannon', jumping to premature actions and conclusions. As a result, they can sometimes make the wrong decision, which can then be difficult to shift. They are more comfortable working with other judgers, as perceivers tend to hold them up. To be effective, salesmen need to be able to articulate their arguments quickly and concisely, making an impact early.

Perceiving types tend to be flexible and spontaneous. Plans and structure tend to inhibit them. They will prefer to adapt to situations as they develop. Meetings will tend to be informal and will often over-run. Journalists are often perceivers.

Selling to perceiving types can be frustrating. They will often be reluctant to make decisions, preferring to prevaricate, especially if they have received conflicting advice.

Salesmen working with perceivers need to give them time and space to work things through in their own time. Salesmen are advised to avoid, as far as possible, asking a perceiver to make a big decision. Where this is not possible, it can be effective to turn large decisions into a series of smaller decisions, which are easier to take. Also, giving the perceiver time to edge towards a decision will often be more effective than pressurizing him to take it before he is ready.

Individuals of a similar personality type tend to communicate and work effectively together. Sometimes, two individuals feel themselves to be 'on the same wavelength' – this frequently happens when there is a good match between personality types. By contrast, different personality types can clash, especially when there is a strong leaning towards the extremes. If the salesman is unable to adapt his behaviour to accommodate his client's personality, it may even be appropriate for the vendor company to assign a different salesman to that client. The successful salesman will be willing and able to recognize and adapt to his client's personality style, with a view to improving both business and personal relationships.

COMBINATIONS OF PERSONALITY TYPE

A full MBTI analysis will categorize individuals according to their location on each of the four Jungian personality axes, giving a total of sixteen possible categorizations. This model is too complex for most people to carry around in their head, so many simpler models have become popular in the business world.

Much of the attention of the management scientist has centred upon the thinking–feeling and sensing–intuitive axes. Haley and Stumpf have studied how positioning on this matrix can affect the way a manager makes decisions (Haley and Stumpf, 1989). Sensing–thinking types, for example, tend to ignore qualitative data, and new data and procedures, tending to rely rather too much on standard procedures. They tend to be analytical and logical in their approach to work, paying great attention to detail. Intuitive–thinking types ignore contradictory information, and over-emphasize positive confirming data. Sensing–feeling types over-emphasize value-laden and emotional information, and go with majority views. Intuitive–feeling types over-emphasize successful outcomes, incline to over-simplification, and can jump to conclusions on inadequate data.

In our case study, Chris Newton, International Consulting's salesman, has attempted to guess the personality type of all the key decision-makers at Global Life. Whilst it should be stressed that these are not rigorous MBTI assessments, the process of thinking about a client's personality type can be helpful to the salesman in understanding the client better. The examples on pages 61 and 62 illustrate Newton's estimate of Simon Nutt, systems manager, and of Mike Chadwick, IT director.

NEURO-LINGUISTIC PROGRAMMING

Neuro-linguistic programming, or NLP, was derived from work in the early 1970s by American academics Richard Bandler and John Grinder, based at the University of Santa Cruz, California. Their early work dealt with verbal and non-verbal communication. It provides a prescriptive model to improve communication and to promote personal change. It is of value to the salesman, because it provides a set of procedures and techniques developed to influence and change the behaviour of others.

O'Conner and McDermott (*Principles of NLP*, 1996) state that the first and foremost principle of NLP is 'rapport', as applied to relationships between yourself and others. They suggest that everyone sees the world differently, because of differences in upbringing and experiences, and that, in order to gain rapport with others, we need to acknowledge them and their view of the world. They suggest that rapport can be established or broken at many different levels, through body language, voice tone

---

PERSONALITY TYPE ASSESSMENT FOR SIMON NUTT

I estimate Simon Nutt to be an ENTJ.

Extrovert (E):
Nutt enjoys talking, and the company of others strongly extrovert characteristics. He regularly calls meetings of his own staff, and invariably spends a large part of those meetings, addressing the group. He is open about his ideas and has a wide range of interests both at work and in his private life.

Intuitive (N):
Nutt readily associates with the top management's vision of diversifying from insurance products to more broadly based financial products. He is attracted by creative and imaginative ideas, such as our suggestion to integrate a new product engine into our back-office streamlining proposals. He is excited by the prospect of helping to turn the firm's fortunes around. By contrast, he is irritated by his manager, Chadwick, who focuses on delivering a service today, and has a habit of criticizing what Nutt sees as trivial detail. These are characteristics of an intuitive personality type.

Thinking (T):
Nutt is relatively analytical and logical strong thinking traits; however, he is also a good people manager and is sympathetic, so exhibits feeling traits as well. Whilst his type on this scale is much more balanced, I have estimated his preference is a thinking style because, when confronted with a tough decision, his head rules his heart. For instance, having tolerated the situation for several months, he recently reprimanded an employee for a prolonged period of unsatisfactory performance, despite knowing that the individual concerned had been going through a messy divorce. He is liked and generally regarded as reasonable and fair by his sub-ordinates.

Judging (J):
Nutt is well organized, methodical and likes to plan ahead. He makes decisions easily and, once he has made a decision, tends to stick with it. He is continuously frustrated by Chadwick's sitting on the fence, forever asking for more information to put off making a decision. These are strongly judging characteristics.

---

and choice of words. Spoken or written language is the most common communication medium. However, research has shown that, when body language conflicts with verbal information, we usually attribute more significance to the non-verbal information.

Consider the following example. You have received this e-mail from your immediate manager: 'Thank you for your report on departmental inefficiencies. Let's discuss it before distribution. I would like to make some of the conclusions considerably sharper.'

PERSONALITY TYPE ASSESSMENT FOR MIKE CHADWICK

I estimate Mike Chadwick to be an ISTP.

Introvert (I):
Chadwick is a quiet, dour man. He takes a deep interest in his work and will often reflect long and hard on issues before venturing an opinion. He is not naturally sociable and keeps himself to himself. He brings a packed lunch to work each day, rather than eating with colleagues in the canteen. He is an obsessive e-mail user, and often writes ten or more notes a day to each of his reporting managers. He is married, but is private about his family life.

Sensing (S):
Chadwick is obsessed by detail. He relies heavily on facts and likes well-reasoned arguments. He becomes quickly irritated by any unsubstantiated assertions made by the sales team, and seems to see the back-office project as primarily a cost-cutting exercise. So far, he has shown little inclination to embrace our suggestions for a new product engine.

Thinking (T):
Chadwick is very analytical, and rarely displays emotion. His management style is to criticize rather than encourage, and he seems fairly insensitive to the feelings of those who work with him. He is not particularly liked by his colleagues, but is viewed as fair by most who know him.

Perceiving (P):
Chadwick is not particularly well organized. His desk is usually cluttered with manuals and correspondence, and his meetings regularly start late and over-run. He always wants to understand every angle in any debate, and even then will often ask for more information before reaching a decision. Once he has made a decision, he often changes it.

Without any additional information, such a message could reasonably be construed as a criticism of the report.

Now consider the following scenario. Your manager drops into your office. He has your report under his arm. 'Thank you for your report on departmental inefficiencies,' he says, smiling, and sticking out an upraised thumb. 'Let's discuss it in more detail before distribution,' he adds, nodding his head towards the office next door, then raising his eyes to the heavens. This office is occupied by Jim Clements, who has come in for some veiled criticism in the report. 'I would like to make some of the conclusions considerably sharper,' he says, pointing conspiratorially towards Clements' office.

Interpretation of body language alongside the text places a very different meaning on it. The non-verbal messages override the verbal.

NLP says that we communicate, often subconsciously, in many ways other than verbally. We also use the position of our body, facial expressions, especially the eyes, and the animation of our movements. Even skin colour or breathing patterns can give away internal emotions. If we can learn to interpret the information flowing through these additional communication channels, we can build rapport more effectively.

One method by which a salesman can improve rapport is by matching body language and voice tone with those of his client. This is a particularly effective way of acknowledging the presence of the person who is the target of the vendor. Matching seating position, eye contact, posture, limb positions and hand gestures can convey powerful subconscious messages of rapport and communication. Matching can also be achieved by using similar voice tone, voice speed and verbal patterns. Within close or intimate relationships, when a couple are in harmony with each other, matching often happens automatically. Neither partner is necessarily conscious of their matching behaviour, but the overall effect is to increase trust and rapport between the two.

Mismatching is the opposite of matching. If you want to break off a conversation, mismatching can signal a break, without a word being needed. Standing up, sitting back, looking at a watch, or even looking away can signal the end of a conversation. Mismatching can provide a less intrusive method of breaking a discussion or meeting.

Matching establishes a link to another person, which, once established, can be used to lead. If a client becomes angry or excited, a salesman can appear more responsive by matching body language, perhaps acting with urgency and appearing tense. Such behaviour acknowledges the client's emotional state, and expresses some rapport with it. It is likely to be more effective in defusing the situation than, say, leaning back in a relaxed fashion. Having established a matching link, the client can be gently led down to a less agitated state. This may be achieved through the gradual relaxation of body posture, slowing and deepening of the voice, and lessening of hand movements – as well as choosing the right words, of course!

SUMMARY

This chapter is, of necessity, selective in the models it discusses. Psychology is a wide and diverse science, and models other than those described here do exist. The value of any model is that it provides a vehicle for looking at an issue in a different way; for stimulating ideas that might be useful or innovative in a sales environment. Whilst none of the models provides a definitive statement as to how to build a relationship with a client, they all provide a framework within which to consider a client's motivation, personality, needs and behaviour. They may also act as a useful guide to discover why particular relationships are not developing well. They may be useful in considering the level of detail to include in calls and presentations, and in judging how hard to press for a decision in the sales campaign.

Overall, the models provide a useful tool for the salesman to reflect upon the client's behaviour, as well as upon his own. If, by using a particular model or theory, the salesman can place a mirror in front of himself, to learn how others perceive him, he is closer to being able to adapt his own behaviour in order to build more effective client relationships.

Salesmen who understand their client's behaviour and adapt their behaviour accordingly, are salesman who are well equipped to build powerful relationships; these relationships will stand them in good stead when buying decisions come to be made.

KEY POINTS

- Ensure our proposals:
  - satisfy and motivate the client;
  - reward the client;
  - meet the client's needs.

- Understand the client's personality type.

- Adopt a behaviour that enhances our relationship with the client.

- Use and interpret body language to understand and influence the client.

5

POSITIONING STRATEGY

There is a tide in the affairs of men
Which, taken at the flood, leads on to fortune;
Omitted, all the voyage of their life
Is bound in shallows and in miseries.
On such a full sea are we now afloat,
And we must take the current when it serves,
Or lose our ventures.

Julius Caesar, Act IV Scene 3
William Shakespeare (1564–1616), dramatist

INTRODUCTION

This chapter looks at the practicalities of positioning a proposal. Combined with the relationship strategy described in Chapter 6, it forms the basis of an overall campaign strategy.

Our case study has now moved on a few of weeks. During that time, partner Barbara Turvey and Chris Newton, the salesman, have made many calls on different client personnel. They have gained an understanding of the environment, and some of the key management issues at Global Life. They have started to unravel the decision-making process the client will go through and identify the interests and buyer values of the key players in the decision-making process. They have also started to understand some of the complex political games that are going on as a result of the new senior management appointments. Our senior consultant on the sales team is Linda Porter. For this sales campaign, she is managing a team of three consultants. The four of them have become immersed in understanding Global Life's current products and processes, and the plans that the firm has for developing into new financial markets in the future.

We have also taken Simon Nutt to see our work at National Mutual. The visit went extremely well, and, following his report, the technical evaluation team of Chadwick, Jones, Guest and Nutt again made a successful visit to National Mutual immediately prior to releasing the RFP.

International Consulting has recently received the formal Request for Proposal, or RFP, from the Global Life Insurance Company (*see* page 67). We were pleased to see that our efforts in suggesting that Global Life considers enhancing its product engine have been successful. Not only is the subject included in the request, but it has also been given a high degree of prominence.

PRIMARY OBJECTIVE

At any point in a sales campaign, it helps to have a clear view of the likely end point, or *primary objective*. This may, of course, change with time. Selling a complex solution may involve many iterations on both sides. Having members of the same sales team with different views of the primary objective can be a recipe for chaos and confusion. At any given moment, all members of the sales team should have a clear and common understanding of the primary objective. Furthermore, whilst the primary objective may change only occasionally, each time it does, the whole sales team should be drawn together and re-briefed on any new direction for the campaign.

The primary objective will need to be reviewed occasionally during the campaign to check that it is still relevant. Generally, it will remain unchanged throughout. However, a shift in the client's requirements, or subtle changes in the objective, can result in major switches of campaign tactics.

Figure 5.1 shows the primary objective Barbara Turvey has set for our sales campaign to Global Life.

CRITICAL SUCCESS FACTORS

Once the primary objective has been set, the core members of the sales team should be brought together to define the critical success factors (CSFs) that need to be addressed in order to deliver that primary objective. The generation of CSFs is best performed by a facilitated brainstorming session involving all members of the sales team. Fifty or more ideas can come out of this exercise, which can then be grouped into more generic CSFs and prioritized. A list of four to eight CSFs is ideal. If there are more than eight, the list tends to be an unfocused 'catch-all'; on the other hand, if there are less than four, the team may be missing some important factors.

Mr M. Chadwick
Group IT Director
Global Life Insurance Company
1 Alpha Crescent
London

Barbara Turvey
Partner
International Consulting
1 Convent Street
London

1 November 1996

Reference ww/mc/357/1996/pj

Dear Barbara

Request for Proposal

Your company is invited to submit proposals for a new back-office system for Global Life Insurance for implementation in time for the new millennium.

Global Life's recent market performance has improved significantly. We achieved double-digit revenue growth last year. Global Life is particularly strong in the Life and Pensions market, where our existing products have taken market share from major competitors. We now wish to build on this performance, by rationalizing our product set to meet the new challenges presented by the continued convergence of the financial services market.

Your proposals are invited for a streamlined back-office system, for implementation by spring 1999. These proposals should show cost reductions over our existing operations. You may also include any suggestions you have for helping us rationalize and develop our products as the firm diversifies into other non-insurance financial markets. Details of our existing and planned product developments are included in the supporting material, along with details of the computer equipment we have installed. Your observations regarding improved business processes and work-flows are also invited.

Your proposals should conform to the format detailed in the attachments. You are invited to submit twenty copies of your tender on or before 16 December. Proposals should be sent to Mr Oliver Smith, clearly marked 'Back-Office Proposal'.

Between now and 16 December, we will be holding a number of briefing sessions and dialogues with all suppliers invited to submit a proposal. We are interested in your views of recent developments in the market, and how your company has solved these problems for other clients in the financial services market. Please find attached our detailed requirements.

Should you have any further queries, please contact Mr Oliver Smith in the Procurement Department.

Yours sincerely

M. Chadwick
IT Director

> ## PRIMARY SALES OBJECTIVE
>
> To sell a new back-office solution to Global Life by
> 1 May 1997, for delivery by spring 1999.

Figure 5.1: *Primary sales objective*

In our case study, Barbara Turvey and her sales team of Chris Newton, the salesman, and Linda Porter, the senior consultant, have taken some time away from the office to plan the rest of the sales campaign. The chart on page 65 shows the CSFs the team has created to achieve its primary objective at Global Life.

The CSFs will often not change significantly during a campaign. However, they should be revisited from time to time, to ensure that the whole team is still focused on the right issues. Should the primary objective change, the CSFs should all be re-evaluated and modified in the light of the change.

Having generated the CSFs, the team will need to turn to those key activities that need to be undertaken in order to address them. The first group of tools will help build a positioning strategy. (Chapter 6 looks at tools to help develop a relationship strategy.)

POSITIONING A BID

The supplier's needs

In positioning a bid, you will need to be cognizant of both the client's needs, and, equally importantly, of the needs and capabilities of your own business. You will need to understand what your company can deliver, within what time-frame and at what profit margin. Some of these factors will be pre-defined for the sales team. At all times, it is important for the sales team to remember that any private-sector organization exists primarily to make money for its owners and shareholders, and that closing a deal that makes a loss, or that cannot be delivered in the desired time-frame, does not best serve the interests of those stakeholders. In the heat of the campaign, it is easy to forget that winning bad business can be worse than winning no business at all.

Chapter 9 on deal-shaping looks at this subject in detail. As in other areas of selling, the problem is to shape a deal that meets as closely as possible both the supplier's objectives and those of the client. At this stage, the salesman needs to understand that any proposition he places

---

CRITICAL SUCCESS FACTORS

1. Ensure there is a business case for the work we propose. Focus the client on the value of our proposition not just the price.

2. Understand what competitors are bidding for and what their strengths are.

3. Identify key decision-makers; and the decision-making process.

4. Build relationships with key decision-makers and identify their key buyer values; find out what relationships we already have with Global Life within International Consulting's senior management.

5. Understand how the client's decision will be evaluated and made.

6. Articulate and sell our strengths, especially in project delivery and change management.

7. Leverage our recent work at National Mutual, especially the introduction of a flexible product engine to allow for the rapid introduction of new products.

---

in front of the client will need to be conditioned by the needs of his own business, and that that may well constrain his ability to bid precisely what the client wants.

Differentiating a proposal

It is important for you to differentiate your offering from that of your competitors. However, differentiation is only of use if the client attributes value to it. Simply finding differences is not enough.

There are two tools for positioning an offering, in order to highlight relevant differences from the competition – the SWOT and killability analyses. From these are derived the *key messages*, which form the basis of any sales campaign strategy.

SWOT

Operating within the constraints of its own business objectives, the supplier's first positioning activity is to perform a SWOT analysis. SWOT stands for strengths, weaknesses, opportunities and threats. It is the most fundamental tool for determining a positioning strategy. It summarizes how the vendor stands with respect to the client and the competitors. Strengths and weaknesses are essentially inward-looking, where the supplier looks at its own organization and what it can offer relative to its competitors and to the client's requirement. Opportunities and threats are external to the immediate situation and to the requirement. Opportunities are new factors that the supplier or the client may introduce into the equation to improve the supplier's competitiveness; threats

	Internal	External
Positive	Strengths	Opportunities
Negative	Weaknesses	Threats

Figure 5.2: *SWOT*

are new factors that a competitor or the client might introduce to improve their competitiveness. Strengths and opportunities form an armoury of positive reasons for the client deciding in one supplier's favour. Weaknesses and threats are the negatives that will need to be handled, and minimized (*see* Figure 5.2).

It is important to make the SWOT relevant to the situation. A list of miscellaneous strengths that the vendor may possess is of no value if they have no relevance to the client.

A good SWOT analysis will have three or four entries under each heading. Its objective is to focus thinking, not to provide a catch-all covering every possible eventuality. A poor SWOT will contain a long list of strengths, and only one or two entries under each of the other headings. Whilst such SWOTs may serve to bolster confidence, their use is limited. A SWOT with more equal weighting to all four quadrants will offer a more balanced perspective from which to make useful strategy judgements.

Attention to opportunities and threats can be particularly rewarding. Opportunities can provide an insight as to how the vendor might change the campaign battleground by stressing new areas where the company is stronger than its competitors; threats can forewarn of likely competitive initiatives. Figure 5.3 offers an example of a SWOT relating to International Consulting making their bid to the Global Life Insurance Company against a number of other consulting organizations.

From the SWOT, the supplier company should determine whether its bid is optimally positioned. Look in any bookshop – its bestsellers are on display in the window; best-selling records are listed in the charts in record shops. It is an old military adage that effort is more effectively applied by building upon strength, rather than attempting to repair weakness. The same applies to sales campaigns – the more the salesman can move the argument towards building upon his own company's

STRENGTHS	OPPORTUNITIES
Our understanding of insurance industry	Leverage our relationship with National
Delivery capability	Mutual
Change-management capability	USA visit to demonstrate our global
Track record in insurance, especially	insurance competence (re-position us as
National Mutual	innovators)
WEAKNESSES	THREATS
Lack of strong relationships with client,	Taurus Consultants may offer freebie
especially Weaver	scoping study (standard practice in their
Access to Global Life's top	last three bids)
management	Price seen as more important than value
Technology competence	
Price	

Figure 5.3: *SWOT relating to international consulting bidding to Global Life*

strengths, the better. Clients select suppliers for their strengths, so the supplier should endeavour to define the battleground in such a way that its bid is positioned to play to its strengths. Time spent rationalizing to the client why those strengths are the most important is well spent. The SWOT may highlight areas of the bid that should be stressed because of a particular strength. Creativity will be needed to argue why those areas of strength should be given a greater weighting in the decision-making process. One approach may be to arrange visits to clients where those particular strengths have led to projects being an overall success, and these should be incorporated into the campaign plan. Other approaches can include customer testimonials, the views of unbiased external experts (industry-watchers, press articles, books and even academic papers), and straight assertion.

Despite that military adage, weaknesses may also need strengthening. In an extreme case, this may mean partnering with another firm, which can bring additional resources or competencies to the solution. Sound commercial judgement and client feedback will be crucial here; advice regarding how different teaming arrangements might be viewed by the client should be sought before any major decisions on sub-contractors and business partners are made. Some clients like working with loose consortia, despite the potential problems of accountability and control. Others insist on a single party taking prime-contractor responsibility for a contract, and this may involve the supplier taking on business risks over which they have less than perfect control. In all of these considerations, the vendor should be guided not just by their own sound business judgement, but also by the client. Decisions relating to business partners concern the client too, since both companies will have to work with the business partner in the future. Sales advantage can certainly be gained by involving the client in any partnering decisions.

Competition and killability analyses

In formulating SWOT and CSFs, the vendor will have been aware of its competitors, and their likely lines of attack. A killability analysis will focus on a specific competitor and lead to the vendor directing its messages more accurately, in order to distinguish its solution.

As with the SWOT, the objective of a killability analysis is not to 'knock' the competition. Direct criticism of competitors is frequently counter-productive; after all, the client has, in his wisdom, invited those competitors to bid too. To criticize a competitor is to question the client's judgement in considering the competitor's proposals, and this is not a clever tactic when trying to win a client's trust. Also, the client already knows that a supplier is bound to be biased in favour of its own solution. Any disparaging remarks about a competitor will be discounted and may be viewed as cheap. As a general rule, criticizing the competition is a dangerous game to play and rebounds unfavourably more often than it succeeds. If, despite all this, the supplier decides that competitive failings *must* be brought to the client's attention, it should be done just once, forcefully, unemotionally and as factually as possible.

The objective of a killability analysis is to get the client to focus on areas of your strength and your competitor's weakness – to change the battleground so that it is more advantageous to you. It does not attempt to disparage the competitor directly, but leads the client along a path that will cause him to reach the conclusions you want him to reach of his own accord. This fine dividing line, between disparaging a competitor and altering the battleground to your own advantage, is of critical importance in the corporate selling environment. It represents the difference between questionable practice and good salesmanship, and can have a major influence on how the client views you and your professionalism. You do have the right to advise the client what you think is important in his decision and where your company is strong. But you advise the client where your competitor's failings lie at your own peril.

A killability analysis forces you to put yourself into the competitor's shoes, to think through what their key strengths are, and what they are likely to be saying about you. Such information may not be on your files, and some creativity may be needed to understand how competitors are likely to act. Possible sources include your own knowledge of the competition, other salesmen who have contested sales against the same competitor, and ex-employees of the competitor company. Other customers of the competitor organization may be able to provide useful information. In all cases, the currency of the information source is important. Whilst companies tend to display specific characteristics and to specialize in certain market segments, their characteristics can change with time. Over the past decade, for example, many of the major mainframe-computer manufacturers have developed competencies in consultancy and services; many of the major consultancies have developed and improved their selling capability.

Once the competitor's likely behaviour has been defined, you need to think how you can combat or refute each of their 'killer' messages about you, and what positive advantages you can develop to encapsulate your response. The resulting list of advantages can then be tested against your key messages, to ensure you have enshrined sufficient competitive positioning in them.

Killability analyses are particularly effective in a two-horse race with another strong competitor; they can serve to sharpen your messages, to differentiate your offerings, and to present your solution in the best possible light relative to that competitor. The example on page 74 shows a killability analysis for International Consulting against Bunch Computers, a large US-based multi-national that has recently committed many hundreds of millions of dollars to entering the consulting business.

Key messages

Having determined the positioning of the bid, with the help of the CSFs, SWOT and killability analyses, the vendor should determine its *key messages*. These messages will form the theme of the sales campaign; they will be included as part of every call brief produced, in every presentation made to the client, and in all formal written proposals to the client. Key messages provide a campaign with a consistency of message crucial to establishing the bid's identity and character. They will serve to differentiate the bid from others, by highlighting the parameters believed to be crucial to ensuring that the bid is selected.

Drafting the key messages is an important activity. The SWOT will help in defining those areas where a bid is naturally strong and can provide a good starting point for writing. Coaches within the client company can fulfil a useful role in helping the supplier understand those messages that will be well received by the decision-makers. Key messages are more powerful if they relate directly to client benefits – statements that simply relate facts do less to further the cause. The following would be a weak key message: 'International Consulting is good at delivering projects on time.' A better key message would be as follows: 'Because International

KILLABILITY ANALYSIS

INTERNATIONAL CONSULTING vs BUNCH COMPUTERS

BUNCH'S LIKELY SALES APPROACH TO SELLING AGAINST INTERNATIONAL CONSULTING

Stress their strong brand and global organization
Emphasize their strong historical relationship with Global Life Insurance Company (as their technology supplier)
Highlight their financial strength, balance-sheet assets and depth of resources
Leverage their capability as a major technology manufacturer

THEIR KILLER MESSAGES ABOUT US

1. International Consulting, as a consultancy rather than a manufacturer, does not understand technology.
2. International Consulting is a partnership with few assets, which makes them financially vulnerable should the project fail, and therefore a high-risk supplier.
3. International Consulting has no loyalty to or relationship with Global Life; Bunch has an existing relationship with Global Life Insurance Company through supplying computer hardware for many years.
4. International Consulting is expensive.

OUR RESPONSES TO THEIR KILLER MESSAGES

1. As International Consulting does not manufacture technology, our recommendations will lack vendor bias.
2. International Consulting has $1 billion annual professional liability insurance, and a higher credit rating than Bunch Computers, so is not a high financial risk. International Consulting's delivery track record is very successful. The business risk with International Consulting is therefore minimal.
3. International Consulting understands Global Life's business, having worked with similar-sized insurance companies in recent years. International Consulting can become a true business partner to Global Life, bringing best industry practice to operational problems.
4. International Consulting aims to deliver optimal business value, not lowest-cost proposals.

INTERNATIONAL CONSULTING'S KILLER MESSAGES

Bunch Computers does not have a track record of solution delivery.
Bunch Computers has little knowledge of the insurance industry.
Bunch Computers does not posses strong business-change credentials.
Bunch Computers are box manufacturers; they will be biased in their technology recommendation.
Incorporation of a new product engine into the functionality of the back office will deliver additional business value unique to our proposal.

KEY MESSAGES

1. LOW BUSINESS RISK
International Consulting's core strengths are those that will minimize business risk:

    – track record of delivery of projects on time and within budget;
    – business change;
    – innovation in the financial services industry.

2. VALUE DELIVERY
Because International Consulting delivers on time, we will partner with Global Life to deliver measurable net business benefits to Global Life from 1 January 2000.

3. VENDOR INDEPENDENCE
International Consulting is technology-independent, and therefore best able to advise Global Life on technology procurement, and on techniques to avoid vendor lock-in.

4. COMPETITIVE EDGE
Our proposals will deliver a state-of-the-art back-office solution to offer Global Life Insurance improved competitive edge through:

    – lower transaction costs (cost base will be reduced by at least 30 per cent);
    – higher revenues, through enabling the faster introduction of new financial products;
    – offering a better, more responsive service, leading to higher customer satisfaction.

Consulting delivers on time, positive business benefits will flow to Global Life from 1 January 2000.'

Once drafted, the key messages should be well understood by all members of the sales team. Posters on workstation walls and notice-boards can be helpful *aide-mémoires*. The key messages should always form part of call briefs for every call, and the calling executives should understand what is behind each one. Whilst many calls may be arranged to cover specific topics not directly related to key messages, every call represents an opportunity to build an overall identity. Consistency of message from each calling executive can be powerful in reinforcing that overall image. As an additional benefit, inclusion of the key messages in every call brief can also serve to ensure that the call's objectives are in line with the overall campaign strategy.

The list on page 75 lists a set of key messages appropriate to International Consulting in their bid to Global Life. The messages are all stated as positives, but also address the negatives identified in the killability analysis. Notice also that we have picked up the client's stated request for innovation (*see* page 67), as this may be a clear differentiator against Bunch Computers.

SUMMARY

Using these tools, the bid has now been positioned, taking account of the supplier's business objectives, what the client wants, and what the competitors are likely to be saying. At present, the positioning of the offering is defined to the client through the key messages. These will later be incorporated into tasks, but first there should be a pause in proceedings.

At this point, a judgement needs to be made as to whether the approach represents a winning strategy. If it does not, the bidder should decide whether to withdraw from the contest before large sums of money are spent on a sales campaign. It is much less painful to withdraw from a bid early than to lose a long and expensive campaign six months later. A well-directed sales-force can reduce a company's overall cost of sales significantly. Focusing effort on winnable opportunities and reducing the cost of sales accordingly, allows a company to make either larger profits or to become more competitive through reducing prices – both of which are desirable in the long run. Any decision to withdraw early should be accompanied by a senior-management review of the reasons why this decision was judged appropriate. From such a review, opportunities for future product or service development may emerge, allowing the supplier to improve its competitiveness in that market next time around.

Having built the positioning strategy and decided to contest the situation because it is potentially winnable, the sales team is now in a position to turn its attention to the next element of the campaign – the relationship strategy.

KEY POINTS

■ Understand the client's environment and problems.

■ Define the sales objective, and the actions necessary to meet it.

■ Define the playing area to:
  - ■ exploit our strengths;
  - ■ expose our competitor's weaknesses.

■ Differentiate the solution in ways that offer value to the client.

■ Base the campaign on a few important key messages.

6

RELATIONSHIP STRATEGY

A man, Sir, should keep his friendship in constant repair.

A Life of Johnson
James Boswell (1740–95), lawyer and writer

INTRODUCTION

Some years ago, I was asked to advise on a sales campaign. The manager responsible for the campaign introduced me to the sales team. The lead salesperson was a Spanish woman with little command of English. She was a brilliant consultant, but, because of her lack of language skills, her ability to build rapport was limited. Her right-hand man was a German, who spoke some English, but was difficult to understand. The lead technician was a very intelligent woman, who lacked communications ability, and the final member of the team was a newly appointed, abrasive young manager, on a fast track to senior management. This group of four had already been introduced to the prospective client's top management team. The prospective client, a medium-sized company, was located in a rural backwater. The management had an average age of fifty-five, and some had been with the firm for decades. The managing director was a former naval frigate commander, and very formal; women had yet to feature in his management structure. There was also a strong sense of xenophobia within the firm.

Throughout the sales campaign, communications were poor and relationship-building was difficult. We had failed to take account of the type of people with whom we were dealing. We had not put relationship-building considerations at the top of our list of priorities when putting the team together.

Time spent early on planning how relationships will be managed can repay itself many times over, in terms of improved team performance, better relationships forged with the client, and overall co-ordination of the project. In my experience, the relationship strategy for a client is the most crucial element of any campaign plan. Chapter 3 looked at how to go about building relationships. This chapter is more concerned with the relationship *strategy* – who to build relationships with and the mechanics of managing relationships within the client company.

ORGANIZATION CHART

The starting point for building the relationship strategy is the client's organization chart; the more comprehensive this is, the better. It is used to identify the key senior managers within the client organization. Such charts are usually fairly easy to get hold of – often they are posted on employee notice boards or circulated in in-house magazines. For government departments and most large organizations, they are published; even if they are not, it is usually possible for the salesman to ask someone to explain the client organization for him.

The organization chart is important for several reasons. It shows each individual's position within the organization. It shows the line responsibilities within the organization and who reports to whom. It shows how the organization is structured and how the various administrative functions within the organization are grouped.

At the top of the organization chart is the chief executive officer, or CEO. He is usually the most important and influential member of the client organization. It is also likely that he will be involved with, or at least aware of, any major procurement involving the expenditure of company money. A good relationship with him is likely to be very useful. If he is doing his job properly, he should want to know and trust the organization with which his own company is dealing.

The salesman should carefully consider who is to be the CEO's main contact within the selling organization. In a small company, the salesman's immediate manager may be the right person; in a larger one, it may be appropriate to involve a board member or, in the case of a very large organization, the vendor's CEO himself. Whoever is chosen, that individual should be prepared to fulfil the role of 'executive contact manager' for a reasonable period of time – at least a year and, ideally, longer. These relationships are so important, many sales organizations now manage the executive contact with their important clients as an ongoing programme, regardless of the specific sales opportunities. If a relationship with the CEO exists, it enables the selling organization to call out major issues at short notice if an emergency occurs during the campaign.

A strong personal relationship between senior representatives of the client and vendor organizations is the single most important factor in building a winning sales strategy. It is a prime responsibility of the sales-campaign leader to ensure that sufficient energy and attention is expended by his organization, to ensure that such a relationship is built and maintained throughout the campaign.

The organization chart will also highlight other key players. Where there is to be major expenditure, the financial director will usually want to satisfy himself that the business case is robust. The marketing director may be required to deliver additional business volumes as a result of the solution being bid; his commitment to the business benefits may be critical to the successful authorization of the bid. Key user groups may also be evident from the chart. In all cases, a relationship between appropriate individuals within the vendor and the client company may be valuable when the buying decisions are made.

The key point about an organization chart is that it highlights those individuals with the line responsibilities within an organization. By careful study of all the top managers on it, it should be possible to ascertain who ought to be involved with the buying decisions that affect the proposal. The individual at the head of each of the functional groups involved in the decision is likely to be a valuable ally during the decision-making process.

A simplified organization chart for Global Life is shown in Figure 0.2.

POWER MAP

Chapter 2 covered sources of power and where it lies in different types of organization. The salesman needs to bring that intelligence to bear, along with his knowledge of the client, in order to construct the organization's power map for the sales campaign.

The power map is an important tool for the analysis of who influences whom within the organization. It is distinct from the organizational chart, in that the lines of influence it depicts do not necessarily follow formal organizational lines. A power maps recognizes that decisions are not always made within formal structures, but that certain groups of people, or cliques, talk together and influence each other. By understanding an organization's power map, it is possible to influence key players, to whom you may not have easy or ready access, through people who do influence them.

Figure 6.1 is an example of a power map for the Global Life Insurance Company. Note that it is titled 'Power Map for Global Life's Back-Office Decision'. Power maps are always situation-specific – different executives will have different power profiles for different decisions.

Start by identifying the key decision-maker, and place him near the centre of the power map. In the Global Life example, Colin Weaver, the CEO, is the key decision-maker. The people who report to him or influence him are placed in bubbles around him, with the number of lines

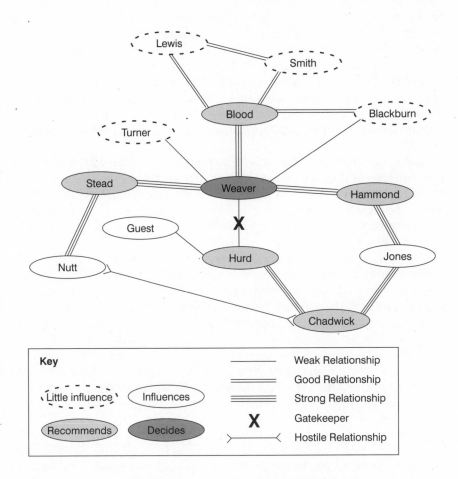

Figure 6.1: *Power map for Global Life's back-office decision.*

between each bubble depicting the level of influence each has on the other. (In a more complex version of the power map, which some find useful, two sets of lines can be used, with arrows depicting the level of influence in each direction.) Three lines represents a strong, close relationship, where there is mutual respect and reliance between the executives. Two lines indicates a good relationship, with a fair degree of trust and support. One line depicts a weak relationship. Maybe they talk to each other on civil terms, but there is no great personal rapport between them. The absence of a connection indicates relationships where there is no known influence.

Further bubbles are added and linked into the key decision-makers, recommenders and influencers, until there is a complete power map for all the client personnel involved in the buying decision. Note that not all the executives on the organization chart are included on the power map – only those believed to be involved with this specific decision are included. The power map may be shaded, to highlight those players who may play a key role in the decision-making process. This can indicate the decision-maker(s) (those who make the positive decision of who to choose as a supplier), recommenders (those who formally advise the decision-maker) and influencers (those who influence the recommenders and deciders).

Other refinements to the power map include the indication of hostile relationships and of gatekeepers. Back arrows, as shown between Nutt and Chadwick, are used to denote hostile relationships. An 'X' on the line(s) denotes a gatekeeper – a person who controls access to another, more senior person. In this procurement, Hurd expects us to contact Weaver through him.

Completion of a power map needs a considerable amount of intelligence information about relationships within the client company. Building the map is a judgemental process, and there is no right or wrong answer. Its construction may also change over time, as the organization changes and relationships wax and wane. However, construction of a power map need not be done in isolation, for colleagues and other observers of the organization will have views on where the power lies. In my experience, many client personnel are happy to help construct such a chart relating to their own organization and are more than willing to give their own views on where the decision-making power lies.

Once the power map has been constructed, time needs to be spent interpreting it. If a senior executive is accessible and he tends to be supportive at all times, there may be little point in devoting effort to building relationships with his influencers. Alternatively, if there is a key executive who is difficult to reach, attention should be given to those who influence him, with a view to getting the message across through these intermediaries. The power map will also tend to highlight those people in an organization who appear to have very little influence on others, and those who have great influence. Clearly, time spent developing relationships with the latter will provide greater leverage than time spent with those who keep to themselves.

We have been advised that the formal recommendation line to Weaver is from Mike Chadwick, via deputy managing director Richard Hurd. However, Hurd has a weak relationship with Weaver. The background to this is that Hurd is a long-time Global Life employee, with over thirty years' service to the company, and had been CEO-elect two years earlier.

Following disastrous results, Weaver was brought in a year ago, to turn the company around. Weaver immediately delegated the second-tier functions to Hurd and focused his efforts on the two key functions that he judged needed special attention – finance, and sales and marketing. The two men do not get on and Hurd is expected to retire shortly. Apart from Hurd, Weaver has surrounded himself with new brooms. Blood to run finance, Hammond to run sales and marketing, and Stead. Stead is Weaver's appointment in Hurd's empire, and his job is to manage the firm's long-term strategy, as well as to keep an eye on Hurd! Stead is expected to succeed Hurd after his retirement. He recommended and helped to recruit Nutt to the firm, to fill the job as systems manager in Chadwick's organization. The chairman, Turner, is non-executive and Weaver keeps him at arm's length. He is only likely to have a mild influence on any decision.

It is far from clear to International Consulting's sales team who will ultimately influence Weaver the most on the Global Life decision. Chadwick and Hurd are both long-term Global Life employees. Both will need persuading, as they will be making the formal recommendation. Chadwick is fairly indecisive and does talk to his team. Jones is a close personal friend and confidante, and Chadwick listens to him most. Guest and Nutt also report direct to him, and, with Jones, make up Chadwick's formal evaluation committee. Weaver will almost certainly ask Stead for a view, as he will soon inherit the programme as Hurd's replacement.

Stead plays golf with Nutt at weekends and their wives are great friends. Stead is godfather to Nutt's daughter and the families used to go on holiday together when the children were younger. Nutt is highly ambitious and is expected to rise rapidly within the organization. It will therefore be worth ensuring that both Nutt and Stead are supporters of our proposals. However, since his recruitment, Nutt's relationship with Chadwick has deteriorated, so that it is unclear how much notice Chadwick will take of his views when making his formal recommendation. Blood and Hammond are also likely to have a say in the final decision; Blood holds the purse strings and Hammond is the main internal customer for the new back office. Our main calling list is therefore: Weaver (decision-maker), Blood, Hammond, Stead, Hurd, Chadwick (likely recommenders), and Jones, Guest and Nutt (main influencers). These are all depicted on the power map by lozenges with a solid line outline.

In interpreting the power map, it is important that International Consulting directs its relationship-building efforts where they will have the greatest impact on the final decision. Sales resources are limited, and focusing on the important players is crucial if the decision is to be won.

MARKER LISTS

Once the key players have been identified, the sales team needs to decide who in their own organization should develop relationships with those players. Marker lists or marker maps can be used for this purpose.

Marker lists are used to define who on the vendor's side is the *marker* responsible for relationships with individuals within the client. It also records an assessment of the client's attitude towards the vendor's proposals.

Care needs to be taken in constructing a marker list. As resources are limited, it is essential to target those individuals who are germane to the decision-making process – either directly or through the influence that they exert. Regular reference to the power map will be necessary during this process, in an attempt to cover every important player involved in the process, and recognizing that some relationships will work better than others. Client individuals who are involved in the decision, but ignored by the vendor, are likely to interpret the vendor's actions as viewing them as unimportant to the process. Even if this is the case, it is wise not to generate such feelings, as these people may well negatively influence others who are important to the decision process.

Next, the vendor needs to ensure that the right pairings are made, with due sensitivity to organizational level, buyer values and personality type. Each of these has been covered in detail earlier; close attention to them is at the root of successful relationship-building. In a multinational environment, you also need to be sensitive to the wider issues of culture and nationality. For example, a US company with a small locally based Japanese subsidiary, making a sale in Japan, needs to consider whether it is more appropriate to match local Japanese staff to the client's chief executive or to use more senior US executives. The US executives will carry more line authority, but the Japanese managers many find it easier to communicate and establish a stronger working relationship.

Regular assessment of the attitude of each individual within the client company to the proposal can provide a useful management tool. It may lead to identification of cliques of support and resistance; both of these are useful in determining actions that may need to be taken during the sales campaign. It may also provide evidence of changes in people's attitudes towards the vendor, as the client discusses the proposals and opinions start to form.

Figure 6.2 shows a typical marker list for our case study example, illustrating against each client executive the name of our marker, estimates of the client's personality type, and assessment scores over time (+2=very positive towards International Consulting's proposals; +1=positive, 0=neutral; −1=negative; −2=very negative).

Global Life Executive	Title	Personality notes	International Consulting's marker	Initial assessment 3/3/97	Current assessment 3/5/97	Last call
Weaver	CEO	Not known	BRT	?	?	–
Hammond	S&M Dir	ENTJ	CDN	0	+1	15/11
Blood	FD	IST?	LWP	+1	+1	11/11
Hurd	Deputy MD	?SFP	CDN	0	–2	18/11
Stead	Strats & Plans Dir	INTP	BRT	0	+2	11/11
Chadwick	IT Dir	ISTP	CDN	0	–2	25/11
Nutt	Systems Mgr	ENTJ	CDN	?	+2	25/11
Jones	Computer Mgr	ES?P	CDN	?	0	28/11
Guest	Applications Mgr	ISFP	CDN	+1	+2	21/11

Figure 6.2: *Marker list*

Note that, following a series of calls in late February, our perception of the individuals' attitudes towards us has changed significantly. In summary, the 'old guard' grouping of Hurd, Chadwick and possibly Jones, appears to be unsupportive towards us. By contrast, Weaver's 'new brooms' – Stead, Hammond and Blood – seem to be positive, and Stead's friend Nutt also seems happy to dissent from his management's negative views of us. It has emerged during calls that the old guard appears to want to retain the status quo of Bunch Computers; the new brooms, however, believe that a change of supplier is necessary. Understanding that this power struggle is going on will be crucial to the way in which we manage the campaign going forward. It may mean, for example, that the technical merits of either our arguments, or those of Bunch Computers, will have little bearing on the final decision, as positions seem already to be well entrenched.

The marker list also highlights another issue. Are we being as smart as we could be on our marker mapping? We judge that Hurd and Chadwick tend towards being introverted, sensing, feeling types. They are quiet, sensitive people, who work hard and conscientiously, preparing detailed papers for decisions. They are also concerned about the effect that our proposals will have on their people; some of our business change proposals have been particularly badly received, since they involve many job changes and some redundancies. International Consulting's salesman, Chris Newton, is a highly extrovert, intuitive thinker. Whilst not exactly thick-skinned, he has, on occasions, been accused of insensitivity. Could our alignment with the new brooms, plus a possible personality conflict, be giving rise to the hostile reaction we are getting from Hurd and Chadwick? Might it make more sense to get Chris Newton's manager, Barbara Turvey, to call on these individuals instead? She is a more introverted, sensing type herself and is a good people manager. She might be better able to generate a more compatible and sensitive relationship with Chadwick and Hurd.

The final point that flows from study of the marker list is that we have not yet got to Weaver. If, as we surmise, he is the final decision-maker, and if there are two competing factions beneath him, we need to understand where he himself is coming from. A plan to get to Weaver is now badly needed if we are better to understand how to play our cards over the weeks leading up to the decision.

BUYER VALUES CHART

The buyer values chart lists those key items that motivate or interest each of the major decision-makers, approvers and influencers. It should be reviewed and updated after each call, and should be used in call planning to shape how future calls are directed and managed.

WEAVER
Forward-looking
Revenue growth
Efficiency
Relationship with analysts and
  investment fund managers

HAMMOND
Revenue growth
Service to customers

BLOOD
Cost reduction
Efficiency
Ambition to succeed Weaver

HURD
People impact
Likes detail
Unconvinced of need for change

STEAD
Forward-looking
Revenue growth
Long-term view

CHADWICK
Likes Bunch Computers
Concerned for his people

NUTT
Upward-looking
  (beyond Chadwick)
Ambitious, and looking for next
  promotion

JONES
Wants to please
Likes detail
Upward-looking
Does as he is told

GUEST
Interested in people
Very technical
Likes detail

Figure 6.3: *Buyer values chart*

The buyer value chart can provide the sales team with a focus. It serves to remind them of the individual's reasons for buying. Figure 6.3 shows a buyer value chart for our case study example.

RELATIONSHIP STRATEGY

By use of the tools described, the vendor should have determined the following:

❑ who the key players are and upon whom the sales team should focus its relationship-building efforts;
❑ who is responsible in the vendor organization for developing relationships with key client personnel;
❑ what the key players' buyer values are.

These assessments, updated and refined after each call, provide an ongoing definition of the vendor's relationship strategy for the sales campaign. In combination with the positioning strategy, they will provide the sales team with the basis for managing the sales situation.

KEY POINTS

■ Understand the client's organization and where the power lies.
■ Understand who will participate in the supplier decision.
■ Mark the key client personnel with the right people on our team.
■ Monitor and manage the key relationships.
■ Understand and sell to their main buyer values.

7

SITUATION MANAGEMENT

The Romans did what all wise rulers must: cope not only with the present troubles, but also with ones likely to arise in future, and assiduously forestall them.

The Prince

Niccolo Machiavelli (1469–1527), statesman and political theorist

STRATEGY AND TACTICS

During World War Two, the strategists of the Allied Forces believed that it was imperative, when shelling enemy positions, that the infantry should push up as hard as possible behind the shelling lines. As soon as the shelling ceased, the infantry could move in rapidly and clean up any small remaining pockets of resistance, before the enemy had time to regroup and marshal its resources. The harder the infantry pushed up behind the shelling line, the more successful the ensuing mop-up operation was likely to be, but speed was of the essence. If the enemy troops had time to recover from the artillery's bombardment, their resistance could be fierce and lethal.

The only problem with a strategy of pushing hard up behind the shelling line was that not every shell landed precisely where it was meant to. One in every few thousand shells would land well short of its target and fall in amongst the Allies' own front-line infantry troops, with horrific consequences for those soldiers in its line. The dilemma for the advancing infantry troops was clear. Should they trust the artillery and push up hard for a ruthless and rapid kill as soon as the shelling ceased, or hold back, avoiding the odd bad shell, but having much more exposed, uncovered ground to traverse once the shelling stopped? The former course of action was strategically the better option and the military commanders knew that it would lead to the smallest loss of Allied life overall; however, from the perspective of the infantry troops on the front line, the choice was far from clear-cut.

An effective sales campaign needs to marry strategy and tactics into a focused plan of actions. This is where sales campaigns most often falter.

There may be a lack of efficiency in the sales process, with the most basic of messages taking too long to get through to the client in a convincing manner. Where there is an inefficient communication process, people do not always receive the message that the speaker means to impart. And there will always be activities that no one has the time to perform.

The supplier organization is looking to create a favourable impression, yet creating an impression that matches reality can never be taken for granted. The sales campaign plan needs to focus the activities of the selling organization in the most effective manner, to concentrate activity on the key levers, and to build the most important relationships.

This chapter discusses some tools for bringing strategic and tactical plans together into a unified sales campaign.

THE CASE FOR IMPLEMENTING A SOLUTION

For any sales campaign to succeed, the sales team has to win two major decisions:

❏ to proceed with the solution at all;
❏ to proceed with that sales team's solution, rather than with the solution of any of the competitors.

Most of the vendor's attention will be directed towards the second of these objectives, and in practice it will consume most of their energies. However, before embarking upon a lengthy and expensive sales campaign, it is appropriate to ensure that the client does, in fact, want to proceed. Just because an Invitation to Tender document has been released, or a formal Request for Proposal has been sent out, it cannot be assumed that the client is totally committed to finding a solution. In practice, they may not be, for many reasons. The function issuing the documentation may believe, in good faith, that its organization intends to proceed with a procurement, but a different function, with powers of veto, may not be committed to it. Finance or legal departments can frequently influence a CEO either to defer, alter or scrap a specific procurement.

I was once involved in a sales campaign to sell a solution to an electricity company. We won the decision, but, before the contract was signed, the company suffered a hostile take-over bid. Suddenly, the electricity company needed all its cash to resist the take-over, so the solution was dropped. External factors, such as the loss of a major customer or a new business opportunity, can alter a client's procurement plans. Competition may come in and fundamentally change the scope or shape of the procurement, leading the client company to alter its parameters, to suit its own capabilities better.

At the beginning of the sales campaign it is therefore appropriate to ascertain the level of commitment the client has. At the same time, understanding what latitude there is to alter what has been asked for is important input to the supplier's deal-shaping work.

The client's commitment can be judged according to who has said they wish the procurement to go ahead. If the board, driven by the CEO, has made an unequivocal commitment to proceed, that is probably as strong an assurance as possible that the client is serious. The supplier is still not protected against all eventualities, but at least there is commitment from the top to proceed. Often, however, the procurement will not have this level of sign-off. Typically, a single board executive will be testing the water, to see what different vendors are able to offer. A business case may not exist at this stage and the scope of the project may be hazy. This may not necessarily be all bad news, for it offers the supplier the opportunity to shape the client's requirements to meet its own capabilities more closely; time spent defining the requirement, in order to meet the supplier's organization's own capabilities better, is often the most productive phase of a sales campaign. Some competitors may not participate in this phase of the selling process, and the vendor which does so will therefore have a considerable competitive advantage from the outset.

Before making a serious commitment to expend significant sales effort, the vendor should be convinced that a robust business case exists or can be built to support what is being requested. Without a believable business case, the entire solution is vulnerable to attack from other functions within the organization or to a board-level rejection. If the client is unable to articulate a strong business rationale for proceeding with the procurement, the vendor should seek that assurance at a senior level within the client organization before proceeding. If such assurance is not forthcoming, the vendor should seriously consider whether its efforts are best expended on this opportunity or whether withdrawal from the contest is more appropriate. After consideration of this, if the vendor still concludes that it should contest the sale, assisting the client to build the business case for the vendor's approach should form a major plank of the sales campaign. This can be profitable work in its own right. It can also help the supplier to understand where the important levers lie and where the client will attribute real value to its proposals.

In our case study example, the RFP was issued by the IT director, Chadwick. This fact, and the absence of a business case, was picked up by International Consulting's qualification process. As a result, the client partner was advised to prepare and agree a business case at a more senior level within Global Life.

Having established as firmly as possible the client's serious intent to proceed, the energies of the sales team will then be directed towards positioning its company's bid. This will need to take into account any competitors, as well as the client's needs.

SALES CAMPAIGN PROCESS

Focus

So far the supplier will have considered two broadly based strategies – the positioning strategy and the relationship strategy. The sales campaign plan combines these strategies with a timetable to produce a comprehensive list of actions that, in aggregate, represent the sales campaign process.

Effective selling is not about doing *everything*. It is about focus. Pick the three or four key activities which most need doing, focus on them, and do them well; they then become the centrepiece of the sales campaign and define the vendor's broad approach to making the sale.

A planning session

As a salesman, at the start of a sales campaign, I would take my sales team away from the office for a planning session. For a couple of days, we would endeavour to take a first cut at our positioning and relationship strategies. Two days was rarely long enough, but at least we would make a start and a team spirit would be created, ensuring that we all knew each other and were signed up to the broad thrust of our effort.

The first hour of the first day would always be spent agonizing over what our primary objective was: what was the real business opportunity and did an intuitive business case exist for delivering a solution to it? Once we had agreed a form of words, the rest of the morning would be devoted to critical success factors – attempting to identify what we really needed to do to win the opportunity. The afternoon would be spent identifying the major competitor, developing a simple SWOT analysis, coming up with some key campaign messages we wanted to focus on, and thinking about how to address the competition. By the end of day one, we would retire to the bar, exhausted, weighed down by several dozen untidy flip charts and many more ideas than we could ever hope to implement, and with a sense of too much to do in too little time.

On day two, we would focus on relationships – who we needed to target, who would target who in the organization, and who our enemies, friends and coaches might be. If the session had gone well, I would allocate a few follow-up actions to individuals, before picking up another mountain of charts and calling proceedings to a halt.

I would always leave day three free to deliberate on the creativity and brainstorming of the two preceding days. This was always the most important of the three days. Day three was the day to focus.

An overall approach

In constructing a plan of actions, it is important to have an overall approach to the campaign. This will usually revolve around the supplier's strengths and critical success factors, and the approach should be developed as a continuing theme throughout the campaign. If the sales team has clear differentiators of real value, these need to be clearly articulated.

You may decide that one of your critical success factors is to demonstrate your company's delivery capability. To achieve this, you may take the client to several of your more successful customers, for whom similar work has been delivered to schedule. Using third parties to convey the message can be a powerful selling technique. Visits away from the client's premises also provide a valuable opportunity for increasing social bonds with the client, during meal-times and travel.

Another critical success factor may be to expose more of the supplier's own organization to the client. Visits to corporate headquarters or to research and development facilities, can provide opportunities for the client to meet senior executives and to show off the supplier company in a positive light.

The overall approach to the campaign should take account of all the critical success factors, and build them into a coherent campaign plan, targeted at those involved in the decision. The battleground should be defined in terms of the supplier's strengths, and it should be explained why they are relevant to the client. The overall approach should only be altered if the following happens:

❑ the client advises the supplier that his needs are not being addressed satisfactorily; or
❑ it seems that the contest is being lost, in which case the vendor needs to change tack.

First steps

Armed with an overall approach, I would always document the key elements of the sales campaign plan using the sales tools described in Chapters 5 and 6 – objectives, CSFs, SWOTs, key messages, killability analyses, power and relationship maps. These documents would be built into a binder that became the team's control book for the duration of the campaign.

From these key elements, I would determine the steps we needed to take over the first few weeks, to get the campaign on the road – these might include customer reference visits to plan, laboratory visits to sell and organize, technical work to be completed, presentations and papers to be prepared. I would delegate these actions to other team members, along with deadlines to be met, asking for regular feedback at weekly meetings.

Every sales campaign has a time-scale which can frequently change. If it does, it is usually a slippage. It is easy to create a list of actions to perform in a sales campaign, and then run out of time or resources to execute them all. My approach was to generate a comprehensive list of all the things we could do and then prioritize. By ensuring that the final sales campaign plan contained the most important activities and that these were scheduled into the client's diaries in plenty of time, we were sure to land our best punches. If time or resources permitted, we could start adding those lesser activities thought to be appropriate.

Following up

Each week, I would call the team together and review what we had learnt from our contacts with the client. Following analysis of what we had learnt, I would use the information as the basis for updating the key sales tools in our campaign control book. Had the power map changed? What had the competition been up to? What had the client said to change our activities? Were we on course to win? Each week, we would agree and draw up a new list of actions and put them in place. One additional sales tool I found useful at this stage was the call planner and tracker. This comprised a continuously updated list of all the calls made and planned by individuals from our organization on the buyer organization. It also recorded the key reasons for each call. I reviewed it regularly to ensure that we were calling on all the key players with the desired regularity.

Periodically, we would go back and review the CSFs, and the primary objective.

Figure 7.1 shows the sales process pictorially.

MANAGING SITUATIONS

A lead salesman always needs to spend time developing the key relationships and managing his own sales team. However, the more he can delegate all but the most important tasks, the more time he can spend managing the sales campaign and the sales situations that arise.

I found that having the sales tools up to date and rapidly available was invaluable. If I needed a senior executive to make a call, I could turn out a

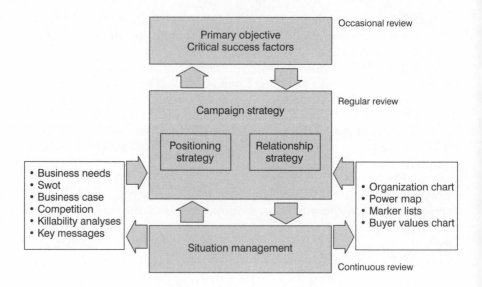

Figure 7.1: *Sales campaign process*

brief in very little time by pulling out the appropriate tools and adding a short covering note. The sales team always understood the strategies in place and pulled in the same direction.

I would usually set up a database for filing reports and write-ups on all the key calls made by each member of the sales team. Each team member would have access to the database and I would ask them to have read the file prior to each weekly meeting. In that way, the team could focus on the key activities, looking forward from a common base of knowledge about the state of the campaign.

Of course, sometimes we would need to react to client situations quickly and before the next full team meeting. Breaking the process on these few occasions rarely caused problems. Having the structure and process in place was an aid to rapid reaction, not an impediment.

A salesman needs to be continuously alert. Information about the sale may not be communicated directly. Warning signs that things have changed include a slippage in the procurement time-scale, a change in client behaviour, or a change in the decision-making process. Time-scale slippage may happen because a competitor has introduced new factors into the evaluation. Silence from a usually talkative and open source may indicate that that source has been found out and warned not to do it again. A change in the decision-making process may precede the client rationalizing a change of heart. The salesman who is alert and sensitive to such signals is better placed to counter adverse developments quickly and to marshal friendly forces in order to get the campaign back on track. In our case study, the campaign has moved on and several key events have now occurred. In early December, a one-on-one call on Global Life's CEO, Weaver, was arranged for International Consulting's managing partner, Jim Bailey. The two immediately struck up a rapport, discovering that they were both keen golfers. Bailey had been briefed to question Weaver's commitment to the project and to stress the business benefits of our proposals. Weaver confirmed that Global Life was committed to reducing costs in the back office, but was also interested in any other ideas we had for further improving the firm's competitiveness. Bailey summarized these as offering Global Life an approximate 30 per cent reduction in back-office transaction costs and the ability to bring new financial products to market rapidly. This second point particularly interested Weaver. Bailey informed him of the work we had done at National Mutual; Weaver listened intently and took some notes. Overall, the call went well. At the end of the meeting, Weaver asked Bailey to let him know straight away if he had any concerns with the procurement.

The proposal writing reached fever pitch during the second week of December. Twenty copies were duly delivered to the client at 4.55pm on 16 December, five minutes before the submission cut-off time.

Over the Christmas and New Year period, Turner and Newton made numerous calls on all the key decision-makers, and it became clear that Chadwick, and his most influential adviser, Jones, were leaning towards Bunch Computers' solution. Nutt informed us that Bunch Computers had put in a strong proposal, offering higher back-office cost reductions than us. Nutt, who was proving an invaluable coach, remained defiantly on our side. Beryl Guest, Chadwick's other adviser, appeared to be fairly neutral; anyway, she had taken three weeks off to be with her family in South Africa over Christmas, so did not appear to be heavily involved in the decision. Chadwick's boss, Hurd, said he would accept Chadwick's recommendation, so we assumed that he too was in favour of Bunch Computers' proposal.

Outside of the formal decision-making process, we were on much stronger territory. Nutt advised us that Stead, Blood and Hammond all favoured our proposal, and that Bailey had made a big impression on Weaver. He also told us that Bunch Computers and Taurus Consultants had both called on Weaver before us and had fared less well. Bunch had stressed cost reduction, but had made no innovative suggestions for further improving Global Life's competitive edge. Taurus Consulting, by contrast, had offered considerably more creative proposals than we had, but had failed to convince either Weaver or Chadwick's evaluation team of their capacity to deliver any of it. Nutt advised us to relax; we would comfortably make the shortlist, although we might have a real battle on our hands after that.

On 15 January, Global Life announced that a shortlist of two suppliers – Bunch Computers and International Consulting – would be invited to submit tenders for their new back-office system.

From now on it would be a two-horse race.

COMPETITIVE INTELLIGENCE

Competitive intelligence is an important subject. In any market where complex deals are contested, the serious competitors will tend to be large, multi-national organizations, with extensive capabilities and resources. This does not mean that they are infallible or that they do not have weaknesses. Every firm has a unique culture, unique capabilities and unique approaches to building complex solutions. The more you can find out and understand about your competitors, the better placed you will be to position your bid.

Sources of competitive intelligence are everywhere. Large firms make news and all are written about regularly. New recruits to your organization may have worked for competitors in the past and may be able to provide insights into their selling behaviour. Customers will often explain in great detail why they like or dislike a given competitor. On one occasion I was shown a manual, produced by a competitor, devoted entirely to sales tactics to be deployed against the very firm for which I was working.

The law surrounding what can and cannot be used as legitimate competitive intelligence is continually changing. It also varies from country to country: data protection acts in Scandinavia are particularly tight regarding the holding of information on specific people employed by competitors; in the USA, the economic espionage act (1996) places restrictions on the collection of data from people who have previously worked for competitors. However, working within the constraints of the tightest legal regimes, good tactical competitive intelligence can arm a salesman with invaluable intelligence. Information on sales tactics adopted, terms and conditions the competitor will or will not sign up for, prices for certain services, and key organizational strengths and weaknesses, can help the astute salesman build a sales campaign that neutralizes the opposition and places his own bid in the best possible light.

SUMMARY

The preceding three chapters have all related to the analysis and management of a sales campaign. It is a complex task, requiring the marrying of both strategic and tactical considerations into daily plans of action. I have found the tools and techniques described here particularly useful.

They help to build a structure around a process that must remain both proactive, to selling the supplier organization's strengths, and reactive, to changes and developments in the sales campaign.

KEY POINTS

- Focus on the key actions needed to win the sale.
- Ensure that the strategy is understood across the sales team.
- Ensure tactics are consistent with the strategy.
- Ensure that the solution delivers business benefits and is competitive.
- Manage the campaign tightly.
- Be prepared to react and adapt to changes in the external environment.

8

COMMUNICATION CONSIDERATIONS

The greatest problem in communication is the illusion that it has been accomplished.

George Bernard Shaw (1856–1950), dramatist and critic

INTRODUCTION

The date: 25 October 1854. The place: the Crimean Peninsula. The British and the Russians have been locked in combat for many months.

Generals of the British Army, based at Balaclava, decide that a gun position held by the Russians should be stormed and captured. Taking it would alter the strategic balance of the conflict, but it is important that it should be taken cleanly and effectively. Cavalry men of the British Light Brigade are dispatched to secure the territory for the British. Misunderstanding the order, the Light Brigade's 'gallant six hundred' attack the wrong position and seize the wrong guns, only to find themselves ambushed by the Russians. There is a wholesale slaughter. Many hundreds of men die that day. Less than two hundred return to tell the tale.

History is littered with examples where communication failures have resulted in disaster. Small but well co-ordinated fighting armies have frequently overturned larger, less disciplined groups. It is the same in selling. Communications are everything. Communicating, both with your own team and with the client, is critical to the success of the campaign. It is only through effective communication that the strategy can be delivered.

COMMUNICATIONS PROCESS

What do we mean by communications? What is the secret of good communicating?

Any communication involves a transmitter and a receiver; that is to say, an information provider and an information recipient. Between humans, this communication process is highly error-prone. We tend to see information in the way we have become conditioned to receive it. Each of us perceives the world according to our experience, personality, background and prejudices. Accordingly, the messages received are often different from the messages that are transmitted.

Take a quick look at the sentence inside the box below. Without dwelling too long on each word, try to count the number of letter 'f's you see as you read. Many adults do not see all the 'f's at the first reading (if you want to check, the actual number of 'f's is given at the end of this chapter). There can be a tendency to miss an 'f' where it is part of 'of', for example, as the trained reading eye tends to pick up the leading edge of a word rather than the trailing edge. However, young children who know their letters but have not yet mastered reading, will tend to pick up more of the 'f's. This is a simple demonstration of a message being distorted or conditioned by experience.

The broader point behind this simple exercise is that, in order to communicate effectively, the transmitter needs to have a good understanding of how the receiver will receive the information being sent.

FINISHED FILES ARE THE RESULT OF YEARS OF SCIENTIFIC STUDY
COMBINED WITH THE EXPERIENCE OF MANY YEARS

JOHARI WINDOW

One useful tool for helping to think about how a client will receive and accept information is the Johari window. This model takes its name from the combined names of its inventors, Joseph Luft and Harry Ingham, and was originally devised as a way of looking at interpersonal communication (Luft, 1969). Figure 8.1 shows a configuration of the window, modified to apply to a situation where a salesman is communicating with an individual from the client's organization about a specific sales situation.

The window has four quadrants. The upper two quadrants relate to the information that the salesman possesses about the situation; the lower two to information of which he is unaware. Similarly, the left-hand quadrants relate to the information the client knows, and the right-hand quadrants to information unknown to the client. There will always be some information known to both sides, and this is shown in the open area (1), or the area of common knowledge. The things that the salesman knows

	Known to client	Unknown to client
Known to salesman	1. Open	2. Hidden
Not known to salesman	3. Blind	4. Unknown

Figure 8.1: *Johari window*

about but has not revealed to the client are in the hidden area (2). Information the client knows, but has not revealed to the salesman is in the salesman's blind area (3). The unknown area (4) relates to information neither side knows.

In a typical sales situation, neither side has all the information they need to know in order to ensure a perfect fit of proposal to requirement. The communication process should endeavour to expand the open area to the point where all the major parameters are agreed, as a basis for the proposal.

Of course, life is not always that simple. In any negotiation, either side may have good reason to withhold information. For example, during the Falklands War, the British negotiated the Argentine surrender whilst the capital Port Stanley was under siege from British troops. The British chose to withhold the information that their ammunition had almost run out and kept this information in the hidden area (2). The Argentinians, believing themselves to be surrounded by troops with overwhelmingly superior firepower, surrendered.

Note that, in this example, the British Army's hidden area (2) corresponded to the blind area (3) of the Argentinians. As the holders of the information, the British had control over whether or not that information was brought into the open area (1).

In a business environment, early in a sales campaign, the vendor may decide to withhold price for competitive reasons. To avoid declaring their hand too early, they may elect to retain that information in the hidden area. When BT, the major British telecommunications company, attempted to negotiate the take-over of MCI, an American telecommunications company, they were initially unaware of the full costs that MCI would need to incur to develop their local exchange network; this information was in BT's blind area. When this hidden information was eventually revealed, the deal faltered, very publicly, and much to the embarrassment of the BT board.

Both blind and hidden areas are inhibitors to reaching a full common understanding. Effective communication techniques can help overcome these and move the negotiations into the area of common understanding.

Finally, there may be unknown factors of which both sides are unaware. When Brian Epstein sat down with the Decca recording company in an attempt to sign a recording contract for the Beatles, neither side had any idea of the success the group was about to enjoy. The negotiations broke down and no contract was signed. The rest is history. Rival record company EMI signed up the group. The Beatles went on to become the biggest-selling pop group in the world and, as a result, EMI became a powerful force in the world-wide music industry.

Any complex relationship has a myriad of open, blind, hidden and unknown areas. One such relationship, with which many of us are familiar, is marriage. Successful marriages are usually dominated by a large open area, for the sharing of common interests and problems can act as a powerful relationship-builder. But there must be few marriages where there are not some hidden areas. The husband who stays behind for a few drinks after office hours may elect to omit the fact that he has had more than one when he gets home. The housewife who is attracted by John Travolta's good looks at the cinema may not over-emphasize her inner-most feelings as she is driving home with her ageing overweight husband. Happy couples navigate their way around the Johari window with some skill, instinctively knowing to which quartile different activities belong, and modifying their behaviour accordingly.

SEEING INTO THE BLIND AREA

Salesmen need to be continuously alert to what may be going on in the blind area. Information deliberately withheld is often held back precisely because it is potentially valuable.

Whilst activity in this area is, by definition, unknown to the sales team, it is often possible to detect warning signs that such activity is occurring. Such signs might include an inexplicable silence from the client, uncharacteristic failure to return telephone calls or messages, excuses to avoid meetings, or any other unexplained changes. Any unusual element in the client's behaviour should set the salesman's antennae buzzing.

Silences from the client can be particularly unnerving and are often indicative that things may be going wrong. In general, clients like giving suppliers good news. It is unusual for a sales team that is about to win a major contract not to have been advised of the fact by someone in the client organization some time before the formal decision is announced. The converse, however, is very different. The losing bidders are frequently kept in the dark before, during and even after the formal decision-making process has run its course.

I used to work for a branch manager who often said, 'If nobody tells you that you're winning, you're not.' As a rule of thumb, it is a good guide. Certainly, if a veil of silence suddenly and inexplicably descends, that is the time to start calling in favours from coaches and friends, in order to find out what is going on. Always listen out for silence.

This aspect of selling has been likened to playing a game of chess with sight of only part of the board. Pieces move in and out of the visible area, and, from that, the player has to estimate what is going on in the unseen areas of the board. Brainstorming possible scenarios within the sales team and then testing them with friends within the client organization, can be a useful technique for gaining an insight into activity within the blind area.

A corporate salesman needs to be aware of the implications of the Johari window and manage his relationships accordingly. Sometimes, clients will pass on information in confidence, requesting him to respect confidentiality, by keeping the information hidden. Sometimes, supporters of competitors will keep information from him deliberately; sometimes he will be unaware of crucial information by genuine omission.

Whatever the reason, the dangers presented by hidden and blind areas can be greatly reduced by establishing multiple close client relationships. Contact levels should also be maintained to such a level as to enable a free and frequent flow of information.

ONE-WAY AND TWO-WAY COMMUNICATION

Some forms of communication are one-way. Traditional television and radio both use one-way communication processes – programmes are broadcast and the viewer or listener receives the information. Here, the transmitter has to decide what it is that the audience wants to see and hear, and provide it. Whilst broadcasting organizations may invest large sums of money attempting to understand what its audience wants, to date, most broadcasting is one-way. The transmitter is taking part in an open-loop exercise – there is little or no feedback on the success or otherwise of the communication until after the transmission.

Sellers occasionally take part in one-way communication. Sending a letter is one example. Making a presentation to a large audience is predominantly one-way communication, although sometimes an audience can make some of its values known to the speaker through applause, heckling, questions or laughter. Writing a book is a one-way process of communication, from author to reader. In all of these examples, the transmitter is sending his message to an audience that has the option of receiving it or not. From the start of the transmission to its end, the transmitter has little idea whether what he has sent is what his audience wants to hear.

One-way transmission is a risky business. Letters are highly targeted transmissions – the sender can usually be confident that it will reach its destination. However, the transmitter has no control over *how* it will be received by the reader, unless he has a good understanding of the receiver's interests. Put another way, the chances that the message will be well received will be greatly improved if the transmitter has some feedback on the recipient before transmission. Television companies perform market research. They are keen to understand how their programmes will be received, so that they can target their product as effectively as possible. They are looking for feedback.

Two-way communication provides that feedback. A telephone conversation is usually a two-way communication. Most conversations between negotiators are two-way – only when negotiations break down is it likely to revert to a one-way process, or 'megaphone diplomacy'. In effective two-way communication, the receiver feeds back information to the transmitter, allowing the transmitter to adapt, usually with the mutual objective of delivering a more acceptable message to the receiver.

Over the course of a sales campaign, effective corporate selling is dependent upon securing an effective two-way communication process between buyer and seller.

The vendor needs to understand what the client wants. The client needs to understand what the vendor can provide. Both have limited room for manoeuvre in order to achieve a match. Prices can be altered, tolerances varied, quality improved, payment terms changed. At a broader level, if the vendor cannot match the client's requirements himself, maybe the requirement can be met by forming an alliance with another supplier. Probably the client does not have a clear idea of what he wants, in which case the vendor may have several choices to make about what solutions to propose.

Corporate selling is a complex business. The business problem under discussion may be messy, and the way in which the vendor's solution is evaluated may be detailed. Gaining an understanding of each other's perspective in such a process is vital to successful selling. Effective communication between the parties involved is also crucial if meaningful relationships are to be developed and a successful sale is to be made.

COMMUNICATION METHODS

In a sales environment, communication occurs by a variety of methods. Each of these methods has different strengths and each is appropriate to a different situation. Selection of the most appropriate communication method should be carefully considered in the light of the particular sales situation.

Letter-writing

A letter is a formal means of transmitting information one-way, without interruption. It also provides an audit trail of what has been communicated and may be used at a later date as evidence of a position taken or a price offered by either the receiver or sender. For one-to-one business correspondence, letters are useful for confirming previously agreed commitments or for communicating salient detailed information that is inherently non-contentious. They can also be used for clarification of an issue that has previously been discussed or for confirmation of a verbal agreement.

Using letters to communicate 'bad news', surprises or reinforce strongly held beliefs is not usually a good idea, however tempting it is. It risks generating irritation or annoyance in the recipient and is unlikely to change the recipient's mind. Not being there to see the annoyance or to handle the issues raised, places the sender at a disadvantage, for two reasons. First, irritations in writing can fester and persist in the mind of the recipient. Once something has been written down, it can be difficult for the sender to modify it or remove it from the sales agenda. Second, the sender gets none of the feedback that is so necessary for effective two-way communication. If the recipient takes issue with the contents of any letter, the sender needs to know about it.

Whilst it may be more comfortable to write from the safety of an office, sending a letter with information you would rather not communicate face-to-face is cowardly, and it will usually be interpreted in that way by the letter's recipient.

Written proposal

As with letters, a proposal is a one-way, uninterrupted transmission of written information, but, in this instance, it has usually been requested by the recipient or buying organization. A proposal may comprise no more than a single sheet of paper, or it may stretch to several volumes and many hundreds of pages. It is effective for conveying the appropriate level of detailed information necessary for the client to assess a proposition prior to making a buying decision.

Being a one-way communication, any proposal contains an element of risk that the contents will not meet the recipient's requirements. It is therefore advisable that, before submitting a proposal, the corporate salesman has put a certain amount of effort into understanding the prospective client's needs as closely as possible; he should have talked through and agreed any contentious issues before the proposal is submitted.

A proposal usually constitutes a legally binding offer. As such, the document will need to be carefully checked and any appropriate disclaimers must be given due prominence. Such disclaimers can highlight areas of weakness in the proposition. For example, the selling organization may not be prepared to pay damages should the solution fail. This may focus the client's mind on risk evaluation, which may not be to the seller's advantage.

A good proposal does not necessarily endeavour to be comprehensive, but should be an interesting read. It should speak primarily to the most senior executives involved in the buying decision, and highlight business benefits rather than products and features.

Presentations

Presentations are a useful method of communicating a complex proposition or idea to an audience of one or many. They provide for a mix of written communication through the use of visual aids, with oral communication. A presentation is primarily a one-way transmission of information, although, particularly with smaller audiences, the audience has a limited opportunity to provide feedback. However, the opportunity to adapt or change position during the course of a presentation is usually minimal. The slides provide a limited audit trail of what is to be communicated. Presentations are useful for painting the big-picture approach to an issue or problem, often to be followed up with written communications on specific points of interest. They are also useful for describing a product or service.

Using presentations to win over a sceptical or hostile audience is risky. It is usually better to tackle dissenters one-on-one beforehand. Whilst presentations may be an effective vehicle for bringing the odd dissenter into line, a hostile audience can undermine and even destroy even well thought-through arguments.

Telephone calls

The telephone has the overwhelming advantage of allowing two people, or sometimes more, to communicate across any distance at any time. It satisfies those two great needs of today: convenience and immediacy. It is because of these strengths that the drawbacks of the telephone are often overlooked.

A telephone conversation is a two-way communication, but it is limited in the amount of feedback it allows. Indeed, many people have a natural aversion to the telephone for this reason; they feel that they need more information on how the person on the other end of the line is reacting, and find the telephone 'difficult' or 'impersonal'. The section on neuro-linguistic programming (*see* Chapter 4) shows how limiting for communication the use of language only can be.

The telephone is not the best method for discussing sensitive or controversial topics. In any situation where the salesman needs to understand how messages are being received, face-to-face contact is preferable. A telephone conversation is also a poor vehicle for the transmission of large amounts of information, and, unless it is recorded, leaves no audit or record of what has been said.

The telephone is excellent for discussing simple uncontentious issues with a small amount of information content. When it is used for other purposes, because convenience or immediacy dictate, limitations of the technology can quickly become apparent.

E-mail, internet and intranet

One of the fastest growing forms of communication is e-mail, with the growth of internet and intranet systems. They are particularly effective for transmitting information, or for initiating actions without a discussion. E-mail technology has many great advantages: the transmitter and receiver do not have to communicate simultaneously; large or small amounts of information can be exchanged; text and pictures can be exchanged; transmission can be made over small or large distances; and an audit trail can be kept by the transmitter and receiver. As telecommunication costs continue to fall, e-mail is also becoming increasingly cost-effective.

There are disadvantages, however. Each packet of information transmitted is one-way, so the reaction of the receiver can only be judged when a reply has been received. Most e-mails are simply text, or text and pictures (although voice and video can be incorporated into the technology). E-mail has often also been cited as an inhibitor to effective relationship-building, with some people even sending e-mails to the person in the office next door to theirs, rather than taking the trouble to walk round for a chat.

One issue that may affect the future growth and development of e-mail relates to the view that the law will take of electronically held and transmitted information. In most Western countries, data-protection legislation is already well advanced and safeguards the rights of the individual whose personal details are held on an electronic database. Legislation is changing fast in the area of electronically stored information, and rules regarding what can be done on such systems are tightening all the time.

In 1997, in a test UK lawsuit, two organizations went to court over the content of internal E-mails. In WPA vs Norwich Union Healthcare, an employee of Norwich Union Healthcare had posted a 'newsflash' about WPA on the firm's internal e-mail system. Norwich Union Healthcare was accused of publishing untrue information about WPA, even though the information was confined entirely to the firm's in-house e-mail system. The offending e-mail information alleged that WPA was under investigation and had ceased to accept new business; allegations that Norwich Union Healthcare accepted in court were untrue. As a result of the case, Norwich Union Healthcare agreed to pay WPA £450,000 in damages. Such an outcome in future may serve to make organizations increasingly cautious and prescriptive in their use of e-mail, even within their internal systems. Ultimately, the rapid growth and use of this type of technology may be inhibited.

Meetings and calls

Of the communication methods discussed, a meeting or a call offers the best opportunity for a two-way exchange of information between vendor and client. It can be the most effective mechanism for understanding a client's requirements, exploring options, and adapting plans, in order to develop an effective solution. It is a good vehicle for delivering bad news, resolving disputes, negotiating a deal, and for building relationships between the participating parties. A meeting can be between two or more people.

Meetings are such an important aspect of the corporate salesman's work that the rest of this chapter is devoted to planning a successful call on a client. (It does not, however, cover sales technique. There are many books and courses on such operational matters as the effective handling of objections, open and closed questioning methods, closing techniques, and other practical aspects of making successful calls.)

PLANNING A CUSTOMER CALL

The customer call is central to the selling process.

The first point to stress about making any call on a client is the import-ance of preparation. Time invested beforehand thinking through the content of the call will be well rewarded. It is far easier to plan the struc-ture and content of a call when you are not under any immediate time pressure. When the call itself is taking place, there will be many other matters to occupy the mind, such as thinking of the next question to ask, and, of course, listening to the information supplied by the client.

Planning for the call should embrace consideration of the caller's objec-tives, which should always be practical, achievable and consistent with the overall sales strategy. The client's likely objectives should also be anticipated. Again, it is far easier to plan how to respond to tough lines of questioning before a call, rather than on the spot during the call itself.

Having defined his objectives, the corporate salesman should plan his likely routes of inquiry. If the call has several objectives, it may be appropriate to make notes for use during the call. Again, against each line of inquiry, he should anticipate likely objections and plan his responses. It is also important to have a clear view of what *not* to say – where he will leave a subject hidden. As with every other aspect of the sales campaign, due sensitivity to the client's personality type, buyer values and level in the organization will need to be uppermost in the salesman's mind when he is planning how to communicate his messages.

Any call has three stages:

❑ opening;
❑ body;
❑ close.

Opening

First impressions count. It is as much a truism as it is a cliché. Making a good impact right at the start of a call can make a big difference to its success or otherwise. Take care to create the right impression. Sensible dress code and hair style, appropriate jewellery, personal hygiene and even body posture are important details that can stand you in good stead.

When meeting a client for the first time, introductions are appropriate. This can be just an exchange of names, but a few words to establish credentials on all sides can be much more effective. As a salesman, when I was accompanied by a technical aide, I would explain their presence with a sentence which also built their credibility within the context of the meeting we were about to have. I might say something like, 'I've asked Mary to come along today as she is the company expert on the design of banking systems. She led our team on the National Westminster Bank project. They have just gone live with a system similar to the one we are proposing to you.'

Another example could be, 'Mike is our expert on customer-billing systems for utilities. He worked on the design of our system for five years, and will be able to address any issues you have on the specification of our product.'

Introductions over, it may be appropriate to exchange pleasantries. This will depend upon the personality of the client. Thinkers tend to want to get down to business straight away and can regard such exchanges as a waste of time. Other, more feeling types may want to relieve the early tension by discussing trivia, such as the weather or the level of traffic getting to the meeting. At this point, the person hosting the meeting should check whether the visitors would like a cup of coffee or tea. Sensitivity to small details can do a lot to reduce early tension levels and prepare both sides for the real business to be addressed.

The final part of the opening should be to remind the client why the meeting has been called. This serves to ensure both sides have a common understanding of the purpose of the meeting, and can identify potential areas of common ground early on. It also sets the agenda for the rest of the call.

Body

The next phase of the meeting is the body. This is where the real business of the meeting is addressed; again, it needs careful preparation. This is the time when information useful to the proposal is gathered, when the salesman will detail his case, and when he should be aiming to understand the client's perspective. Care needs to be taken throughout to ensure that the dialogue is two-way. The vendor should not go in with a fixed and intransigent approach that inhibits the client explaining what they are trying to achieve.

Having listened to the client's needs, the salesman should relate the benefits of his company's approach to those needs. Benefits cannot be articulated in terms meaningful to the client unless that client's needs and buyer values have been understood. Selling features without first understanding the client's needs will do little to enhance the solution's intrinsic worth. By contrast, explaining how a proposed solution or approach can deliver additional client benefits can considerably enhance the appeal of the basic offering.

Key to a successful body in a call is a full and free exchange of ideas and opinion, which serves to expand the open area of understanding for both parties. Effective questioning and objection-handling are important sales techniques that need to be mastered as basic tools of the salesman's trade. Equally important is an ability to listen to the client and to relate to the client's concerns. Whilst there are no rights and wrongs, I would normally aim to get the client to talk for 70 to 80 per cent of the time.

Having understood the client's needs, the solution needs to be linked to the concerns and issues expressed.

Close

The final part of a call cannot be prepared to the same extent as the opening and the body. However, to adopt best practice, there are a few activities that should be performed at the close of any call.

Having addressed all of his initial objectives, the caller should summarize what has been agreed. It may be appropriate to offer to follow up with a summarizing letter, for the benefit of both parties. Any follow-up actions agreed may be defined and an offer made to document these at the same time. Finally, try to find a way of leaving the door open for another visit. Having got into a senior manager's office, it is much easier to agree to return in, say, two weeks' time, with a response to issues raised during the call, than it is to attempt to get into the diary again from scratch. Consider obtaining agreement to fix the follow-up meeting with the client's secretary at the appropriate time.

OTHER COMMUNICATION METHODS

As well as the above communication methods, other, less commonly used methods exist for the conveying of information between buyer and seller.

Voice-mail systems proliferate for internal communication within many firms, but are in much less common usage for communication between organizations. The same is true of video conferencing. Both of these technologies are still developing, and their usage is likely to change in the years ahead.

For many years, video- and tape-recordings have been used to transmit information in a pre-packaged form. More recently, CD-ROM has been used to provide pictorial and spoken information to individual desktops, giving the user the option of branching to areas of particular interest. The fax remains one of the commonest methods of transmitting hard-copy files over switched public telephone networks. Many personal computers now have fax software and hardware built in, embracing the older technology into the new office desktop.

There are many communication methods available to the salesman. It is the task of the salesman to understand the techniques and methods available, to understand their respective strengths and weaknesses, and to select those that are most appropriate to each particular sales situation.

SUMMARY

Communication is the means by which information is exchanged, and the method by which people learn about each other. The more the vendor and client understand each other, the larger the open area and the better chance the vendor has of fashioning a proposition that meets a client's needs. The opportunity for misunderstanding is omnipresent in any communication process. (Did you spot all six Fs on page 99 at the first reading?) Selection of the most appropriate communication method can greatly reduce the chances of such problems occurring.

New technologies will bring new methods of communication in the future. Some will replace existing technologies, whilst others will fail to catch on. The salesman needs to understand the methods at his disposal, along with the strengths and weaknesses of each. Depending upon the information that must be communicated, there are many different methods available.

A face-to-face meeting with the client allows for both the transmission of information and for the receipt of feedback on information transmitted. It is usually the most effective method to use for building relationships, resolving difficult or contentious issues, or for negotiating a deal.

KEY POINTS

■ Communication can be error prone; what you think you have transmitted may not be what has been received. Check for understanding.

■ Effective selling depends upon effective communication with the client.

■ Be alert to activity in the blind area – listen for silence.

■ There are many ways to communicate: letters, calls, meetings, presentations . . . Select the most appropriate.

■ Invest in careful planning for any meeting with the client.

9

DEAL-SHAPING

'The time has come,' the Walrus said, 'to talk of many things:
Of shoes – and ships – and sealing wax – of cabbages – and kings – And why the
sea is boiling hot – and whether pigs have wings.'

Through the Looking-Glass
Lewis Carroll (1832–98), writer and mathematician

INTRODUCTION

I was picking over the entrails of a very dead sales campaign with the lead salesman.

'I just can't put my finger on where we lost it,' he was saying. 'On day one, the client said to us, "Give us your very best advice. That's why we want you on this job. We will never hold it against you." So we did. And we lost. After we had been kicked out we asked what we had done wrong. Do you know what we were told? We were too opinionated!'

The essence of good deal-making is to achieve the right balance, between offering enough of what the client wants on the one hand, and meeting your own business objectives on the other. If the vendor imposes its own views too little, it may fail to protect its own interests; if it imposes too much, it risks being perceived as opinionated and inflexible.

Deal-making can be particularly hazardous for functionally organized suppliers; this is where the different disciplines meet and cross in earnest – sales and finance, legal and technical, human resources and commercial – all with their own views and departmental positions to protect. I have witnessed more suppliers fall apart in disarray at the deal-shaping phase of a campaign than at any other.

This chapter looks first at deal-shaping from the client's perspective, considering the different types of evaluation the client will make during the deal-making process. The anatomy of a deal and the deal-making process are reviewed, and the parameters the selling organization needs to take into consideration when building a solution are studied. Finally, we consider different approaches to deal pricing and the respective merits and drawbacks of each.

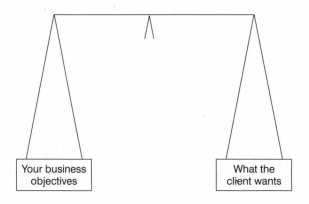

Figure 9.1: *Getting the balance right*

TYPES OF EVALUATION

Whilst there are no prescriptive rules, most procuring organizations will be interested in the following three broad types of evaluation:

☐ a technical evaluation;
☐ a commercial evaluation;
☐ a personal evaluation.

Each of these may be formal or informal evaluations and, to be successful, we will need to be as strong as possible in each area. However, major suppliers are all too aware that raising false expectations can be a recipe for disaster.

Setting an expectation that is too high will leave the customer feeling good – too good – about the deal. Later on, when the reality falls short of the expectation, there will be a major adverse reaction from the customer, and this will probably be expensive for the supplier. It may lead to damage to the supplier's credibility, reduced profitability, or even the loss of the business itself. By contrast, setting expectations too low may cause the client to take a competitor's solution. Clearly, the ideal is to set expectations in line with the reality of what can be delivered. If the reality matches the expectation, long-term client relationships will not be compromised, and the client will have the best possible information on which to base his evaluation of the supplier's offer.

Technical, commercial and personal evaluations are all closely linked. The deal-shaping process needs to balance all three in shaping a satisfactory solution.

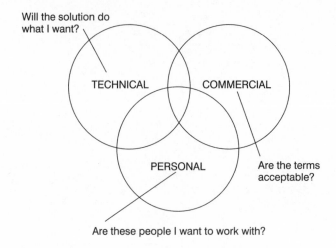

Will the solution do
what I want?

TECHNICAL   COMMERCIAL

PERSONAL

Are the terms
acceptable?

Are these people I want to work with?

Figure 9.2: *Types of evaluation made by the client*

Technical evaluation

The technical evaluation looks at how well the supplier addresses the client's requirements. It will also look at the additional resources and assets the supplier has to commit to the project, should things start to go wrong. The technical evaluation is usually the first of the three evaluations to start, and can be the first casualty when the other evaluations gather momentum.

During the technical evaluation, the client will be looking to ascertain that the bid conforms to the defined requirement, and that the bidder is capable of delivering. Evaluators are likely to be technical buyers, and sales activity will typically involve visiting reference sites and obtaining other client testimonials, to prove technical capability.

The criterion for success following a technical evaluation is for the bid to meet or exceed the client requirements and specification. Technical buyers tend to be the most junior individuals involved in a major buying decision and usually cannot say 'yes' to a contract. They often have the authority, however, to veto a proposal if it fails to meet the technical requirements.

Many technical evaluations are likened to 'clearing the bar' in a high-jump competition – the objective is to clear the obstacle, rather than to clear it by a greater amount than anyone else.

There can be a great temptation to keep adding extras, in the hope of improving a bid's competitiveness. However, extras usually incur additional cost, and, however technically attractive, may either reduce the profit margin or add to the price. Both of these are adverse consequences and should be avoided if possible. It is important to understand how any capabilities that are above the specification requested will be evaluated. The point at which the client agrees that the proposal meets its requirements is the point at which the seller should stop selling or enhancing the solution, to focus on acceptance of the solution.

Watch out for delaying or diversionary tactics from competitors once your technical solution has been accepted. Delay allows other factors to be introduced into the decision-making equation, such as new technologies, new methodologies or new announcements; it allows for other people who may not have participated in the technical decision to be introduced into the decision-making process; it allows for time to elapse between the technical evaluation and the final vendor selection. All of these factors work against the winner of the technical evaluation. They should be anticipated and, where appropriate, the client should be forewarned to watch out for such tactics from competitive bidders. The client should also be encouraged to stick to agreed evaluation processes and timetables, and to communicate the results of the technical evaluation to all other players involved.

Commercial evaluation

The commercial evaluation covers all terms and conditions, financial and legal, that relate to the deal. However, the client will also be concerned with other commercial factors not explicitly covered by the contract, such as the financial robustness of the organization and the confidence the client has in the firm to deliver the goods. Above all of these considerations, the client will take a view on the risk factors inherent in dealing with a specific supplier and the likelihood of the project failing. Supplier organizations need to devote much energy to building confidence, so that potential clients trust them to have the will and the commitment to make the proposed deal work.

Sometimes, the minutiae of the commercial evaluation are left until after all other evaluations; they can be time-consuming and involve a lot of detailed negotiation. At the deal-shaping stage, broad principles will usually be agreed, in the expectation that the final contract will fall within the parameters discussed. The client may wish to discuss indicative prices. If possible, avoid giving these until the scope has been pinned down. Indicative prices can quickly become fixed in the eyes of the client, whereas scope changes are invariably upwards.

A successful conclusion will usually result in an agreement or contract being signed between the two organizations. At the deal-shaping stage, clients are often looking for a specific approach – perhaps a concession on billing rates or a particular level of damages should the project fail. Purchasing departments are often remunerated on the level of discount they can negotiate, and so may have an unhealthy focus in this area, to the detriment of other factors, such as quality, delivery time-scale or risk. Such functions have their place in all large organizations and can deliver real value through negotiation of discounts on commodity products. However, a few adopt a simplistic and confrontational approach to negotiation and this can be detrimental to the deal-shaping process. If supplier and client are to enjoy a mutually beneficial business relationship, the line managements have to be able to talk and resolve issues rather than lean on intermediaries, whose involvement may get in the way of, and damage, the relationship.

Personal evaluation

Much has already been said regarding the importance of relationships with the client company. However, it cannot be over-emphasized that the most important evaluation that the client makes will be of the supplier and its people. With a complex deal, the likelihood is that the companies will be working together for several years once the contract is signed. The client will be keen to ensure that he can work pragmatically and effectively with any supplier. Even if the personal evaluation of the bidder's team does not form part of the formal evaluation process, it will be done subconsciously and will be reflected in the other evaluations.

All the processes and committees in the world will not stop a client placing business with an organization that it trusts and that it knows it can work with. The development of rapport and trust between buyer and seller is at its most critical during the deal-shaping phase of the campaign. Close co-operation at this stage, with each side attuned to the needs of the other, can facilitate the working towards the common objective of a viable business solution.

ANATOMY OF A DEAL

The output of the deal-shaping process is an agreement for both parties to supply resources comprising technology, services and people, in order to meet an agreed set of business goals. There is no standard template for a deal agreement, but it will typically cover most or all of the following topics:

❑ the business need and the business case justification for the programme;

❑ the business goals of the programme;
❑ the scope of the programme;
❑ an outline of the proposed solution;
❑ the resources to be supplied by both sides;
❑ transition plans to move to the client from today's environment to the new;
❑ the time-scale of the programme and key project milestones;
❑ pricing arrangements;
❑ contractual framework;
❑ penalties for non-performance;
❑ conditions under which either side may withdraw from the contract.

In order to reach agreement across these diverse areas, the two sides need to participate in a deal-shaping process. This may be an explicit process or an informal one, with meetings being convened as the situation requires.

THE SUPPLIER'S OBJECTIVES

Before the salesman can start the deal-shaping process, he needs to understand his firm's business objectives. Curiously, these are usually vaguely defined, and may differ from executive to executive within the selling organization.

In assessing the attractiveness of a deal before making a formal tender, the selling organization usually seeks to evaluate the following four key questions:

❑ Can we do the work technically?
❑ What will it cost us?
❑ What are the risks to us?
❑ What rewards can we expect?

These evaluations will be more detailed than those that took place at the initial qualification stage, for the opportunity will now be better defined and many of the softer issues will have become much harder. In most organizations, these questions will be addressed in a formal final management review, before the final tender is submitted to the client.

Can we do the work technically?

The salesman will usually take advice from the solution-delivery functions within his firm. If it has the capability to provide the entire solution from within its own resources, this evaluation will be fairly straightforward. Mission-critical key resources will need to be provisionally reserved for the delivery team. Major technical risks that could compromise or delay solution delivery will need to be identified.

If, however, the supplier does not possess the capability to deliver the entire solution, additional assistance from other organizations will need to be sought. There are two approaches to involving third parties in the deal – sub-contract or consortium.

In sub-contracting, the selling organization takes prime responsibility for the contract with the client, and sub-contracts work to other suppliers when it needs assistance. This approach has a benefit for the client, which has to negotiate with only one organization, leaving responsibility for integration of the solution to the prime contractor. As the prime contractor carries the integration risk, this route is usually more expensive than the consortium approach.

In a consortium, two or more organizations contract, either separately or jointly and severally, with the client to provide a solution. This approach allows the client to select its preferred supplier for each component of the solution. However, it does place responsibility for integrating the solution with the client.

What will it cost us?

Accurately establishing the base-line cost for a deal is critical to ensuring the commercial success of that deal. This is a complex process; in building the cost model, the supplier needs to ensure that all costs are included in the equation. With the best will in the world, it can be easy to miss or understate critical cost elements, which might include items such as management overheads, depreciation costs, project over-run costs, or wrong assumptions on inflation over the lifetime of the project. With global deals, exchange-rate fluctuations can dramatically alter cost assumptions. Often, only the client has access to some cost elements and may refuse to divulge what it considers to be proprietary information, leaving the vendor to incur additional risk in the cost model.

In building a cost model, all costs associated directly with the project should be included. These will include the cost of the people, equipment and services necessary to deliver the solution over the lifetime of the project. Cost of sales should also be built into the cost line; this will involve estimating the direct costs incurred in making the sale – salespeople, lawyers, financial controllers and bid specialists. In addition, the company needs to cover costs incurred in making bids where the business has not been won and the cost of sale has therefore not been recovered. Keeping this amount low will improve price competitiveness. A robust qualification process should ensure that only those situations where there is a strong chance of winning are contested. A high win rate helps to keep this cost apportionment low.

A sensible apportionment of fixed costs should be made for each major bid. However, an approach to fixed-cost apportionment that is too simplistic can ultimately lead to uncompetitive pricing. For example, the selling organization may have a projected world-wide turnover of $1 billion, and a world-wide international management overhead of $20 million, or 2 per cent of turnover. (This overhead is the cost of managing the business and does not involve any project-specific costs.) In building a cost model to bid for a $100 million contract, a $2 million cost for the world-wide management overhead should be included. This will make the costs of that selling organization $2 million more than those of a hypothetical competitor organization incurring no world-wide management cost, and may cause it to lose the business. Losing this bid may cause the organization to revise its year-end turnover projections to $0.9 billion (the original $1 billion, minus the $100 million lost bid). The 2 per cent management overhead will now be 2.22 per cent. Applied as a cost to subsequent bids, this could make the organization even less competitive next time around.

A supplier organization should ensure that its fixed costs do not build to a level that makes it uncompetitive, triggering a downward spiral of increasing fixed-cost overheads and reducing revenues. If it finds that it needs to keep increasing its fixed-cost apportionment on bids, the management of the firm may be better advised to cut its own cost base.

Other fixed costs may be more deal-dependent. For example, in an outsourcing deal, the supplier may be concerned with the transfer of staff from the client to the supplier, where fixed costs for the supplier may include the cost of the additional load on their personnel department. There may, of course, be a corresponding or greater fixed-cost saving made by the client after such a transfer, but only the client organization can realize this.

The supplier's cost model should include all fixed, semi-variable and variable costs, which, in aggregate, build into the overall profit and loss profile for the deal. Failure to understand and allow for the full cost base in pricing deals can lead to incremental profit at margins lower than target. This will dilute the supplier's overall profit profile. Many analysts focus on margin as an indicator of whether an organization is managing its cost base effectively.

The bid's cost profile will typically be built on a spreadsheet, which enables different cost scenarios to be considered and evaluated as the deal-shaping discussions proceed. Building an accurate cost model is crucial for the supplier organization in understanding the flexibility it has to offer deal alternatives to the client.

What are the risks to us?

Any project involves some degree of business risk. With complex deals, these are often significant. Examples of risks to the supplier include the following:

- ❑ the client going bankrupt;
- ❑ the client being unable to pay the supplier's invoices;
- ❑ the programme failing;
- ❑ cost over-runs;
- ❑ sub-contractors failing to deliver to their commitments;
- ❑ sub-contractors going bankrupt;
- ❑ the client failing to deliver to its commitments;
- ❑ scope changes during the delivery of the programme;
- ❑ failure of the supplier to deliver to the client's satisfaction;
- ❑ bad publicity.

Commercial organizations exist to take business risk and to profit from succeeding. This does not mean that suppliers should indulge in reckless bidding, but it is the nature of business that suppliers will need to be prepared to take on a measure of risk in order to win deals. On important and/or mission-critical contracts, the client will often want to witness the supplier sharing in the business risk, as a sign of confidence in its proposals and of commitment to the success of the programme.

Should the client require the supplier to assume a degree of risk, the supplier may expect to be rewarded for carrying and managing that risk. The supplier should only assume responsibility for risks over which it has control. The prudent supplier will endeavour to balance risk and reward, and build in contingency payments to cover risks that may incur greater costs. Such contingency will be used both to reward the supplier, if it delivers to budget, and partially to cover failure to deliver to specification due to circumstances within its control.

One example might be a computer project that has to be delivered to a given specification. The supplier estimates it will take a year to design, build and deliver the project. He decides to commit to delivery within twelve months, as this is the customer's requirement. The customer asks him to guarantee delivery within a year and to pay heavy penalties should he fail to meet the deadline. The supplier re-evaluates the project and decides that, should there be some unforeseen slippage, additional resources will be needed in order to meet the deadline. To cover part of this possible cost, he builds additional contingency into the pricing of the deal. If he manages the project well, he will not incur the extra cost and will reap additional rewards for assuming the risk. If the project slips, he will incur extra cost, but this is at least partially covered by the built-in contingency. In this instance, there is a relationship between risk and contingency which can be used as a basis for making a business decision to proceed with the bid, and for making a balanced risk/reward pricing decision. Typical factors against which it may be sensible for a supplier to build in some contingency might be the estimated hourly cost of a C+ programmer, or the costs incurred for project over-runs, or increased exposure to damages payments.

Risks over which the supplier has no control should not be assumed by the supplier. The logic of this statement is illustrated by the following example: how much risk should a builder of ship's hulls assume? The ultimate customer, a shipping line, wants an absolute guarantee that the ship will not sink, under any conditions. Unqualified, this is an unreasonable risk for the hull manufacturer to assume, as the *Titanic* disaster demonstrates. In that case, the hull had not been designed to withstand the impact of a high-speed collision with an iceberg. Any amount of contingency in the hull-builder's costings could not have guaranteed the safe passage of the *Titanic* on that fateful journey. The disaster was caused by factors almost exclusively outside the control of the hull-builder. Even if the hull had been built more strongly, it is still possible to imagine even more traumatic events that could have caused failure.

In such instances, there is no absolute relationship between contingency and risk for the supplier, as the supplier is not in control of all the risks. Requests to assume such risk should be resisted at any price. Today, some firms will not bid for air-traffic control systems because they cannot be in control of all risks.

The supplier should consider carrying risk only if the following apply:

❑ the risk is well defined;
❑ the supplier understands the risk;
❑ the supplier has a significant control over the risk;
❑ the supplier is the logical and best-placed party to carry or share the risk;
❑ the risk will improve the supplier's chances of winning the sale;
❑ the potential reward is commensurate with the risks being taken on.

There are several types of contractual arrangement which enable the supplier to assume different levels of risk; *see* pages 125–130.

What rewards can we expect?

Whilst commercial companies have multiple stakeholders, diverse missions, different business practices and a myriad of beliefs and principles, they all exist for one primary cause – to generate profit and wealth for their owners. Every deal should aim to make a profit, and, unless exceptional circumstances prevail, should endeavour to maximize profits.

At the simplest level, profit is the difference between revenues received and costs incurred. In order to maximize profit, a company aims to minimize costs and maximize revenues – this is sometimes referred to as 'driving the lines apart'. Costs should be minimized within the context of meeting the customer's functional and quality requirements, and without incurring unacceptable levels of risk. Revenues should be maximized, by setting a price consistent with winning the bid and, again, by not incurring unacceptable levels of risk.

Within this simple analysis, there are many additional parameters to be considered. For example, if the supplier is cash-rich and the major competitor and the client are cash-constrained, the supplier may elect to sacrifice profitability in the early years, in order to secure a strong competitive edge in the bidding process. The deal may be shaped to be cash-positive for the client in every year, subsidizing the contract in the early years and taking a much higher margin in the later years. Overall, this may deliver a winning bid at a greater overall profit than attempting to recover margin early in the contract.

There is no point in a bid delivering a profit several years out if the supplier runs out of cash in the short term. Profits are only profits after the cash has actually arrived in the supplier's bank account. As Azil Nadir discovered during the crisis at Polly Peck, even if profits are increasing, if the cash runs out, the business will go under. Outsourcing organizations, in particular, need to understand the difference between cash and profit: a full strategic outsourcing deal, which involves the purchase of the client's assets and the hiring of the client's staff, is typically cash-negative for one to three years. Without careful cash management, outsourcing organizations can easily become overstretched.

Deal-shapers need to have a good idea of their own firm's strengths relative to those of their competitors and, if it is relevant, play to those strengths in shaping the deal. Trade-offs between short- and long-term cash availability and profitability can be major levers in this respect.

Another key variable is the risk/reward balance. This requires a judgement to be made regarding what degree of risk it is appropriate to incur in order to reap the financial rewards that will flow from a successful delivery. Many firms are risk-averse. Unlimited liability partnerships, for example, tend to find it more difficult to take major financial risks than limited liability companies, because of their financial structure. In shaping a deal, a pragmatic balance needs to be struck, taking into account the needs of the client, the competitors and the attitude to risk of the deal-shaper's own organization.

The supplier may also decide to take a view on the amount of money to be made by managing change during the life of the contract. There is at least one major blue chip organization, specializing in IT outsourcing, which bids at a lower margin in order to win the deal. This organization also insists on very tight scope definitions, in the anticipation of making very high margins on any contractual changes during the life of the deal. Since an IT outsourcing deal typically lasts five to ten years, the chance of scope changes over that time is high; in fact, they are almost inevitable. As the incumbent supplier, the firm is able to command much higher margins for the additional work, as it is rarely practical for the client to invite in another bidder mid-contract.

THE DEAL-SHAPING PROCESS

Having first considered what is wanted from the deal, the supplier is now in a position to start the process of deal-shaping.

It should be stressed right at the outset that deal-shaping is an iterative process. Any attempt to shape a deal in isolation from the needs of the client is doomed to failure.

Figure 9.3 depicts the sub-processes that a typical deal-shaping process comprises. It is an idealized depiction – in reality, the different sub-processes will overlap and there will be some blurring of the boundaries

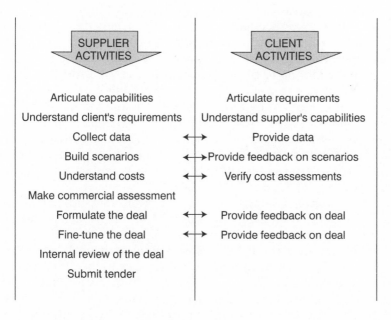

Figure 9.3: *The deal-shaping process*

between the end of one sub-process and the start of another. Most importantly, this figure illustrates the iterative nature of the process (major iterations are depicted by arrows) and the need to involve the client at each step along the way.

The vendor should always start by thoroughly understanding the client's requirements. This involves more than reading the client's written specification. In any deal there will be many undocumented agendas at play. Potential power shifts, career implications and span of control changes, which might come about as the result of a supplier's proposal, will be of intense interest to some individuals within the client. If the outcome of a deal is mission-critical, senior people in the client organization will have their careers on the line: if the deal fails, they will be held responsible, but if it succeeds, they may stand to gain considerably. The salesman cannot ignore these factors, for they will play a part in the final evaluation of any proposal made. Implicit therefore in 'understanding the client's requirements' is an understanding of the broader issues at play within the client organization. Similarly, the client needs to have an understanding of the supplier's capabilities if a meaningful deal is to be struck.

Once the requirements have been understood, there will inevitably be a data-gathering phase. Often, the client will have given the vendor a pre-conceived idea of the shape of the final solution; this will need to be checked out for validity, and challenged if the numbers do not add up.

When the necessary data has been gathered, the supplier will be in a position to build some scenarios; in the early stages, these will be relatively broad-brush approaches to tackling the problem. Testing of these scenarios with the client is a key phase of the deal-shaping process; listening to and adapting to the client's reactions to the proposals is much more important than the supplier's team imposing its own ideas, however crushing this might be to its creative ego. Making the client feel a part of the deal-shaping process is an important element in achieving the client's buy-in and commitment to the proposal. If any individual within the client organization feels that his views are being ignored, that person is unlikely to be a strong advocate of the proposals, however intellectually robust they are.

Once the client has agreed a broad approach, the supplier needs to build a more detailed model and perform a full costing; again, assistance should be sought from the client as appropriate, to ensure that the cost assumptions are accurate. If the circumstances of the sale allow it, the client should be asked to verify the costings, to ensure that there is a common base-line from which the supplier can make its projections.

The costing will form the basis of a commercial assessment of the proposed tender. The supplier needs to ascertain whether the proposed approach delivers a deal that is wanted by both sides. The dimensions of this equation have already been detailed: the client will make commercial, technical and personal evaluations, whilst the supplier will want to take a view of the profits and business risks involved. It is unlikely that all dimensions will be completely satisfied at this point. Again, iterating through different ideas and approaches with the client can greatly improve the tender at this stage. On each iteration, the tuning should become finer, until a deal acceptable to both sides has been fashioned.

Usually the method by which the vendor will be paid is agreed at this stage. This is an important aspect of the deal-shaping process; for details of the pros and cons of differing approaches, *see* page 131.

The deal-shaping process usually finishes with the supplier having a final internal review before the tender is submitted.

PRICING FRAMEWORKS

There is almost an infinite variety of different terms an organization can offer a client. These are usually contained within a framework set of terms, which relate to the method of payment the client will adopt to remunerate the supplier. There are four types of framework, listed below. A deal contract will be based on one or more of these.

Resources used

These contracts charge in proportion to the resources used by the supplier. Examples of resources include people and technology. This is the lowest-risk form of contract for the supplier, as services are paid for as they are used. The buyer carries the delivery risk. However, the supplier is not guaranteed the full value of the contract at the time of signing, as both parties usually have the option of walking away from the deal at any time. Examples of resource-based types of contract are 'Time and materials', commonly used by many professional services

---

DEAL TERMS

RESOURCES USED

TRANSACTIONS PROCESSED

FIXED REVENUE OR PRICE

VALUE-BASED

---

organizations, and 'Cost plus', common to the defence and construction industries.

For the client, resource-based charging will probably offer the best chance of minimizing supplier costs, although this is by no means guaranteed. If the project gets into trouble or is poorly managed by the buyer, such contract costs can soar. A major drawback for the buyer in this type of deal is that the supplier has little incentive to complete the contract early. Contracts in the construction and defence industries are notorious for cost over-runs, usually at the expense of the buyer. To compensate partially for this, buyers often insist upon performance guarantees or offer incentives for the supplier to minimize costs.

Advantages of resource-based agreements are that they offer flexibility for either side to alter the scope of the deal and, for well-managed, relatively straightforward deals, they can represent good value for the client. For the supplier, they usually offer an early break-even point, low financial risk, and a good chance of making a profit.

Figure 9.4 illustrates the financial structure of a typical resource-based contract.

Transactions processed

These contracts charge the client according to the number of transactions handled or processed by the supplier. Examples of the sort of business transaction that might be included in this type of contract are vehicles

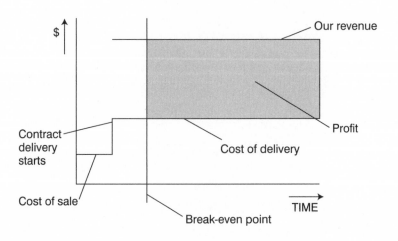

Figure 9.4: *Resource-based deal*

crossing a toll bridge, orders processed by an outsourced back-office function, or the number of reservations made in an airline seat reservation system. With this type of contract, the supplier carries part of the service delivery risk; supplier payments are linked to the number and type of transactions. The supplier also carries the risk of a drop in demand for the service, and may legitimately insist upon certain minimum payments as protection against such eventualities. Conversely, an increase in demand can lead to significantly improved revenues for the supplier.

The client will still carry a major slice of the business risk if the service forms an important part of the overall business operation.

Figure 9.5 illustrates the financial profile of a transaction-based proposal to design, build test and operate a computer-based reservations system, and to charge the client for reservation transactions processed. Note that the break-even point in this example is some way into the future, thereby increasing the business risk to the supplier. Note also that, once profits have started to flow and costs have been covered, the longer the contract runs, the better it is for the supplier.

For the client, transactions-processed pricing algorithms can provide an effective way of turning fixed costs into variable costs. This is attractive to the buyer because costs are only incurred when the firm is generating revenues to cover them. However, if volumes pick up well beyond forecast levels, it can prove an expensive solution for the buyer and lucrative for the supplier.

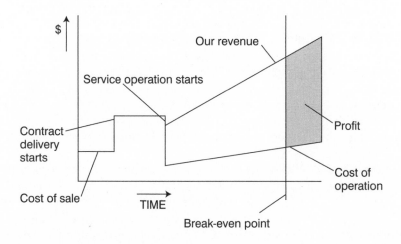

Figure 9.5: *Transaction-based deal*

Fixed-revenue or fixed-price

Fixed-revenue or fixed-price contracts offer the buyer a defined service or solution for a pre-defined price. A typical example of a fixed-revenue agreement might be a maintenance contract for a computer system; according to such an agreement, the supplier will, for a regular payment, service and repair the equipment, as required, to deliver a specified service level. Another example of a fixed-price deal would be for a consultancy organization to provide the design, building and testing of a customized billing system, to be supplied ready to run, for a given price. The fixed price may be paid as a single sum at contract completion. A variation on this approach, which may be adopted in order to ease the supplier's cash-flow, is to take payments as milestones are reached during the project.

Fixed-price agreements offer greater cost predictability for a buyer. However, they increase the business risk for the supplier, for payment is usually dependent upon the delivery of a working solution. In the examples above, the supplier is carrying some external risk; in the case of the computer maintenance contract, one risk is the reliability of the machinery being maintained. A rogue machine could incur significant costs for the supplier. In the case of the design-build-test work, estimating the effort needed to construct the system may be difficult, involving considerable judgement or guesswork. To cover such risks, the prudent supplier will generally charge a premium over and above any estimate for the work to be performed, and may well take out insurance to protect itself against some of that risk.

A fixed-price agreement may appear to transfer much of the delivery risk to the supplier. In complex deals, this may not always be the case, for one major reason – scope changes. Scope changes can work in favour of either party, depending upon how they are handled.

Over the period of delivering a deal, it is almost inevitable that there will be several scope changes. With many deals, scope changes start before the ink is dry on the contract. Over a contract of long duration, competitive pressures and other changes in the external environment, can change the client's needs. Common sense dictates that the contract should adapt to changed circumstances, and both parties have an incentive to negotiate contract changes.

In the case of a fixed-price deal, the supplier may have the upper hand in any re-negotiation, especially if the original scope was well defined. As the incumbent, the supplier will often be offered scope-change work single tender. Incremental work will typically give the supplier the opportunity to increase margins, often significantly. Major scope changes may also offer the supplier some potential for contract extension, although this is more vulnerable to competitive tender.

One risk for the supplier is a client that expects scope changes to be absorbed within the scope of the original contract – sometimes referred to as 'scope creep'. This can increase costs for the supplier, whilst holding the revenue line where it was, thereby squeezing the margin.

One final dimension to consider in a fixed-price contract are the incentives to both parties. The buyer, having committed to a given financial outlay, has an incentive to demand the highest quality possible within the fixed-price terms. The supplier, however, has an incentive to cut costs, as illustrated by Figure 9.6. Every dollar of cost the supplier cuts from delivering to the contract drops through as profit to the bottom line. This incentive can work against the quality objective of the buyer.

Fixed-price deals are sometimes demanded by buyers who take a short-term view of cost, and who have a poor understanding of the business dynamics that make for successful project delivery. In the world of complex deals, the apparently attractive buyer option of a fixed-price deal can break on scope changes or poor-quality delivery, providing attractive options for the supplier.

Value-based

Sometimes, during the selling phase of a campaign, a vendor will offer 'value-based' terms. This is when the seller is remunerated against the client's business performance. For example, International Consulting might offer to take 20 per cent of the cost saving actually realized by implementation of their proposals over, say, a ten-year period. It is important for buyers to recognize that such proposals are often offered as a

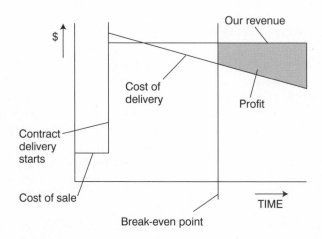

Figure 9.6: *Fixed-price deal*

sales tactic, to demonstrate the vendor's commitment to, and confidence in, the approach. If a vendor makes such an offer, it may well have little expectation that the client will sign up for the proposition, and may not have much desire to sign up itself! Financial and business analysis usually demonstrates that the client will be better off taking the service offered at a fixed price and enjoying the benefit of 100 per cent of the 'value' delivered, rather than sharing it with the vendor.

The vendor, too, will often be relieved not to have to deliver to a value-based contract. Whilst value-based proposals sound fine, writing a contract can be very difficult. Reaching agreement on objective measurement criteria usually proves less than easy. Subjective measures are no good, since there is little incentive for the client to interpret measurements in a manner that increases payments to the supplier. Ensuring that both sides have adequate influence over key business levers can also be a difficult area to negotiate.

As a result, value-based bidding, which can be high-risk for the seller and expensive for the buyer, often gets put to one side once serious negotiation starts. By offering it, the vendor has achieved its goal of demonstrating confidence in its proposals, and, by rejecting it, the buyer has almost certainly lowered the cost of a successful implementation.

The major buyer and supplier benefits, and risks associated with each of these four pricing frameworks, are summarized in Figure 9.9.

AFTER THE DEAL-SHAPING

The deal-shaping concludes with the submission of a tender to the client. This will usually contain an outline of the offer, the proposed terms of the deal and pricing information.

Following evaluation of all tenders submitted, at this point the client normally selects a winning supplier. This marks the end of the buying decision process, and the start of the contract negotiation (*see* Figure 0.1). In many instances, negotiation may already have taken place just to get to this stage, but, from this point on, negotiation will focus on the final contract.

The first step in the contract negotiation process is sometimes the signing of a 'memorandum of agreement' to capture the essence of the deal. This can vary, from a few broad principles agreed by the senior management of both sides, to a mini-contract defining the key parameters upon which the full contract will be based. Subsequent negotiation will focus on filling out the detail of the memorandum of agreement into a full contract.

Another part of the contract negotiation is 'due diligence'. The due diligence process, usually presided over by lawyers, endeavours to document fully the agreement reached. The process aims to define the

DEAL-SHAPING FRAMEWORKS – PROS AND CONS SUMMARY

	Resources-based	Transaction-based	Fixed price	Value-based
Supplier benefits	Low risk (as the delivery risk is with the buyer). Early break-even.	Opportunity to benefit from higher than planned transaction rates.	Potentially higher return (for taking on a higher delivery risk). Additional high-margin business from re-negotiations resulting from scope changes.	Demonstrates supplier's commitment to the client and the proposed solution.
Supplier risks	Buyer has no contractual commitment to a level of spend, and can usually terminate the agreement with the minimum of notice.	The break-even point can be a long way into the future. High project delivery risk, as no delivery means no transactions, which means no payment.	High project delivery risk. All or part of the payment will probably be linked to successful delivery. Scope 'creep' without a corresponding re-negotiation of the price.	High business benefit delivery risk Lack of control over the levers that deliver value.
Buyer benefits	Lowest supplier cost option. Flexibility to alter project's scope during implementation.	What would have been fixed costs are turned into variable costs. Supplier has some 'skin' in the deal as no transactions results in no payments.	Predictable supplier costs.	Commitment to the delivery of business benefits from the supplier.
Buyer risks	Buyer carries all of the delivery risk. Supplier has little incentive to cut costs or complete early.	Potentially expensive if transaction volumes exceed forecasts (although these may be offset by higher revenue for the buyer).	Objectives of supplier (who is incentivized to reduce costs) and buyer (who wants quality) not aligned. Scope changes can be expensive.	Potentially very expensive, as the buyer shares the benefits with the supplier.

Figure 9.9: *Deal-shaping frameworks*

responsibilities of both parties and to specify the recourse each side has in the event of default. Due diligence does not endeavour to introduce new factors into the negotiated agreement – it merely aims to ensure that both sides have the same understanding of what has been agreed and to document that understanding. Due diligence will only be a problem where there have been major misunderstandings during the deal negotiation process.

Of course, misunderstandings can occur during the deal negotiation process. So far, only the *theory* of deal-shaping has been discussed. In practice, any company has to negotiate a deal with one or more other parties. This crucial phase of the sales process is discussed in the next three chapters.

CASE STUDY: SUPPLIER SELECTION

It is now 15 May. Since the shortlist was announced, in January, the deal-shaping has progressed in earnest. Linda Porter and her team of consultants have fully understood Global Life's processes and have built a number of possible implementation scenarios. Chadwick has requested the further analysis of two possible options – the first option, back-office process streamlining, including designing, building and testing of new IT systems to support them; the second option, the same as the first, but with the inclusion of a new product engine to enable the more rapid introduction of new financial products.

Nutt has continued to coach us throughout the period and has advised us that Global Life was now divided over which route to take forward. The 'old guard' of Hurd, Chadwick and Jones was pushing hard for the first option, claiming that to extend the scope of the project further would overstretch the organization. Bunch Computers was making much capital of the amount of change that Global Life was due to experience. In addition to the back-office project, Bunch highlighted the need for Global Life both to introduce new systems to accommodate the Euro, and to alter their systems for the millennium. This, they argued, was enough change for any single organization to cope with at any one moment.

The 'new brooms' of Hammond, Blood, Stead and Nutt all favoured the second option. Nutt advised us to argue that, given the amount of change necessary, the firm might as well accept that many of its IT systems needed a re-write from scratch, and that now was an ideal time to introduce an integrated new product engine. The divide within the firm was ideological, and Nutt advised us to submit two tenders, making option 1 as competitive as possible, as Bunch Computers planned to bid only for that option. He also told us that, not only were Bunch Computers claiming they could make reductions similar to ours, but also that, from conversations so far, their fees were likely to be less than ours.

We discussed terms in detail with both Chadwick and Blood, the financial director, offering to perform the work under time and materials, fixed-price or value-based billing terms for both options. Chadwick was particularly attracted by value-based bidding, where we offered to share measurable savings in the cost base with Global Life. Blood, in contrast, wanted to take our services on a time and materials basis, claiming that Global Life would get the same solution from us at a significantly lower price. At one point, Chadwick attempted to argue that International Consulting would be much more committed to the work if we had a financial interest in its success. Blood dismissed this line of argument, explaining that it was Chadwick's job to deliver the system successfully, including management of any supplier they took on. The two men reached an accommodation and requested both vendors to offer a fixed price for any tenders submitted.

A fortnight before tender submission, International Consulting held a final management review. Jim Bailey chaired the meeting and reviewed our proposed tenders for options 1 and 2. Our anticipated margin on option 1 had been reduced to 40 per cent, based on Nutt's advice to us to be as competitive as possible. Our overall gross margin on option 2 was 50 per cent. Apart from Nutt's advice that it would probably be cheaper, we had little idea where Bunch Computers' bid on option 1 would come in.

During the review, Bailey asked why we were bidding for both options. Barbara Turvey replied that was what the client had requested, and this led to a discussion about what we believed was the right solution for the client. Bailey disliked the idea of bidding for such a large contract at 40 per cent margin, but understood the logic of needing to be as competitive as possible in a direct comparison with Bunch Computers. Eventually, he suspended the review and asked Barbara Turvey to arrange for him to see Weaver again, one-to-one, ideally somewhere off-site.

A week later, Bailey and Weaver met for dinner at Bibendum. Bailey described the problem in the following way: International Consulting genuinely believed that the right business approach for Global Life was to take option 2, but Chadwick's process was driving us to bid for option 1 also. We believed that Bunch Computers were likely to undercut us on option 1, as they were desperate for business, and had surplus consulting capacity at present. International Consulting was, by contrast, heavily committed already, and was not keen to bid for this contract at penal margins.

Weaver reflected for some time, then explained his problem to Bailey. 'I want you to win this business and I want it to be option 2. I am not particularly interested in driving every ounce of margin out of your proposals; I just want you in there sorting out the back office. My problem is that I want Chadwick and Hurd out, but not yet. There has been so much change in the past two years that I need an element of stability in the management for some six months more at least. If I overrule them now, they could easily walk out on me, and that could cause me problems with some of the institutional investors. I will have to give some considerable weight to their recommendation unless I have very strong counter-arguments.'

The two men discussed various options and agreed a course of action. International Consulting would submit two bids. For option 1, we would bid very low. For option 2, we would bid our normal margin. In addition, we would commit our strongest possible team to the job, including assigning the client partner, Barbara Turvey, full time to manage delivery of the project. Only the two men would understand that our option 1 was not real; International Consulting would walk away from the deal if that were selected. It was a plan that required trust on both sides. Bailey judged that he could trust Weaver.

On returning to their offices the following day, both men set the wheels in motion. Weaver sent a note to Hurd stating that he wanted to review his recommendations for the supplier for options 1 and 2. He also said that he wanted a full board meeting to review whether Global Life should opt for option 1 or 2, regardless of any supplier implications.

Bailey called Barbara Turvey into his office and explained why she should submit a bid for option 1 at cost, but that the gross margin on option 2 should remain at 50 per cent.

On 1 May, Global Life made an announcement that International Consulting was their partner of choice for their back-office project. Their stock rose several points on the announcement. Two weeks later, following a board meeting, Hurd called Barbara Turvey with the news that the board had made a unanimous decision to go with option 2. He had the authority to initiate design work immediately and wanted to sign a memorandum of agreement as soon as possible. Contract negotiation could proceed in parallel with the work.

Jim Bailey called Colin Weaver to thank him personally for his involvement in the process. Both agreed that they were well satisfied with the outcome and looked forward to a long and mutually beneficial business relationship.

They also agreed to play a round of golf together at the end of the month.

KEY POINTS

■ Understand the client's objectives.

■ Understand our own business objectives.

■ Aim to win the technical, commercial and personal evaluations.

■ Remain flexible and listen to the client during the deal-shaping process.

■ Do not take on risks you do not have control over.

■ Select the most appropriate framework for the deal.

10

NEGOTIATION THEORY

Practice should always be based on a sound knowledge of theory.
Leonardo da Vinci (1452–1519), artist, engineer and scientist

THE PRISONER'S DILEMMA

There is a well-known conundrum that has tantalized game theorists for many years. It revolves around two burglars, whom we will call Alf and Bert. The police have little evidence, but strongly suspect that Alf and Bert have committed a minor crime together. Accordingly, they place each one in a cell and attempt to get either of them to admit that they were involved in the crime together. Figure 10.1 summarizes the options facing each prisoner.

If Alf and Bert co-operate with each other by refusing to implicate each other, both will go free. If, however, Alf co-operates with Bert by keeping his mouth shut, but Bert plea-bargains and admits they were both involved (in other words, he defects), Alf is sentenced to a 15 months in prison; Bert is released and is given a small reward for helping to put Alf away. The situation is mirrored if Alf defects and Bert co-operates. Finally, if both admit to the police that they were both involved (they both defect), then they both receive a five-month prison sentence.

The pay-off matrix in Figure 10.1 reveals an interesting property. Whatever Bert does, Alf is better off defecting. Similarly, whatever Alf does, Bert is better off defecting. Assume that Bert co-operates with Alf, and keeps his mouth shut. If Alf keeps his mouth shut and co-operates too, Alf goes free. But if Alf defects, he not only goes free, but gets a reward as well. Alf is therefore better off defecting. Now consider Bert defecting and telling tales on Alf. If Alf co-operates, he is sentenced to fifteen months in prison. If Alf defects as well as Bert, Alf only gets five months in prison. Hence, from a viewpoint of individual rationality, whatever Bert does, Alf is better off defecting. Similarly, whatever Alf does, Bert is better off defecting.

	BERT	
	Co-operate	Defect
Co-operate	Both go free	Alf gets 15 months Bert is free and receives a reward
Defect	Alf is freed and receives a reward Bert gets 15 months	Both get 5 months

ALF (row label)

Figure 10.1: *The Prisoner's dilemma*

But here's the rub ... *both* are better off if *both* co-operate. Why? Because if, and only if, they both co-operate, both go free. Remember, if both defect, both are sentenced to five months in prison.

This is the 'prisoner's dilemma' – should each one follow individual rationality and defect, or should they trust one another and co-operate?

The answer to the prisoner's dilemma is conditional: if the prisoners trust each other, then there is a good solution to be achieved by co-operating (win-win). Either stands to gain at the other's expense by defecting (win-lose), but the greater overall good is achieved for both by co-operation. If one defects and the other co-operates, it will take a long time for any degree of trust to be re-established between the two. If both defect, then both lose (lose-lose).

In his book *The Empty Raincoat* (1994), Charles Handy relates his extraordinary experiences in workshops, in which he auctioned five-pound notes. He recounts instances where workshop participants would often compete to outbid each other and, in the process, bid well over the face value of the five-pound note in order to win the auction. He also observed that, had the participants co-operated with one another and allowed an initial bid of 1p to stand for the five-pound note, the class could have profited by £4.99 each time a note was auctioned. This is a specific example of the prisoner's dilemma: by co-operating, rather than all attempting to win the auction individually, the class could run at a net profit, which they could then share to the greater benefit of everyone. Where there is aggressive competing, the only winner is the auctioneer.

CO-OPERATIVE AND NON CO-OPERATIVE GAMES

Games fall into one of two categories – co-operative and non co-operative.

Most sports are non co-operative. A football team aims to win at its opponent's expense. A runner endeavours to run faster than any other competitor. A chess player tries to beat his opponent. In all of these examples, there is no co-operation between competitors. Such games are called non co-operative, or zero-sum games; one party wins at the expense of another. In such games, there is no benefit and, in fact, a significant downside to co-operating with opponents. Non co-operative games are confrontational. Other examples of predominantly non co-operative games in real life include war, the trial-by-jury system, hostile company take-overs and the election of US presidents.

Co-operative games are non zero-sum. They rely upon the co-operation of all parties, to achieve a win-win situation. When co-operation, or trust, breaks down, one party can make a short-term gain. However, in the longer term, trust is severely dented, usually making it more difficult to achieve a win-win scenario in the future.

Examples of co-operative games in real life include the GATT agreement on trade between nations, and the use of public transport. In the former, all subscribing countries agree to limit tariffs on the import of the other countries' goods. The win-win means that every country has the benefit of a much larger market to which it can export, without the imposition of penal tariffs. The agreement works until one country attempts to realize a short-term gain, by defecting and raising tariffs to protect its own industry from cheap imports. In the latter example, if everyone could be persuaded to travel to work on buses instead of by car, the roads would be much clearer and the buses would get to their destination much more quickly. Once large-scale defection starts, with some drivers travelling to work in their own cars, traffic builds up again. The win-win situation breaks down.

In the business world, there are many examples of co-operative and non co-operative game-playing. When the British government invited tenders for groups to run the national lottery, they set up a non co-operative contest. However, each competing group of bidders comprised several companies, co-operating with each other in an attempt to build a winning consortium.

The problem with co-operative games is that, by defecting, one party can always achieve a short-term gain. In some instances, that gain may be decisive. Consider the case of nuclear disarmament: everyone agrees to disarm, but one nation defects and secretly develops nuclear weapons, which it is prepared to use. That nation, for the period when it has nuclear weapons and everyone else does not, has an overwhelming short-term advantage. This example is, however, an exception. Most co-operative games are 'multiple-round'. If one side defects, then the other side usually has the opportunity to effect reprisals later, albeit from a weakened position.

Axelrod (1984) states that a long-term strategy for playing co-operative games is 'tit-for-tat'. A tit-for-tat strategy starts by co-operating on round one of a game, and then follows what the opponent has done for each subsequent round. This means that, if one company is adopting a tit-for-tat strategy and the opponent defects, the first company defects on the following round. Such a strategy is clear (it follows an easily understood algorithm), fair (the company only defects if it has been defected against), retaliatory (it punishes defection by defecting itself next time) and forgiving (the company only defects once for each opponent's defection). Over time, the strategy encourages co-operation. In computer simulations, tit-for-tat has proved to be a successful playing strategy in games involving multiple rounds. Many believe that Israel attempted to follow such a strategy against the Arab states during the 1970s and 80s.

GAME THEORY SUMMARY

NON CO-OPERATIVE GAMES	CO-OPERATIVE GAMES
Confrontational	Non-confrontational
Zero-sum	Non zero-sum
Examples: Football War Hostile take-over Trial by jury	Examples: Prisoner's dilemma Nuclear disarmament Public transport Marriage
Individual rationality says defect	Individual rationality says defect
Game theory says defect	Game theory says co-operate
Requires no trust	Requires trust
Best multiple-round strategy: defect on every round	Best multiple-round strategy: co-operate on round one. Only defect when opponent has defected on the previous round (tit-for-tat)

NEGOTIATION

So is a negotiation a co-operative or a non co-operative game?

Your viewpoint can condition your approach to negotiation. In the 1970s, many industrial disputes in the UK public sector were characterized by confrontational, non co-operative tactics. Union leaders would address their paymasters through the media, stating their pay demands. The government would, in similar vein, publicly state government policy. This megaphone diplomacy would continue, until both sides became desperate enough to agree to talks; at this point, both sides would have to climb down from their previously stated position.

Negotiators who adopted this approach failed to understand game theory. Today, we live in more enlightened times. Most major organizations understand that, with co-operation and trust-building, that elusive win-win scenario can often be found. There is also increasing recognition that the achievement of a win-lose scenario, in a large deal with a supplier or customer, risks being a Pyrrhic victory. Often, if the terms of an agreement are so tight that one party loses out badly, nobody wins. A large and complex deal is often mission-critical, and both sides need to be totally committed to making it work. Win-lose contracts do not engender mutual commitment. Trust is the essence of the agreement, and a high level of co-operation is needed to make it work. To this extent, a negotiation is a co-operative game.

However, clearly there are elements of a negotiation that are zero-sum. For instance, many debates around the deal price are zero-sum. What one side gives on price, the other side takes. The same can sometimes be true of other parameters – time-scale, resources, quality and damages are all possible examples. To this extent, negotiations are non co-operative. Understanding when the negotiation is a zero-sum game and when it is a co-operative game, can help to show the way through the negotiation minefield.

Before this theory can be developed further, the dynamics of the negotiation process need to be considered.

THE NEGOTIATION PROCESS

Building on common ground

As discussed in the introduction, a sales campaign will have a 'buying decision' phase. During this period, the sales team is, rightly, focused on winning the sale against its competitors. At some stage during this period a second phase – the 'agreement negotiation' – will start. Here, the focus is different. Negotiation is all about business issues, such as protecting the bottom line, minimizing or controlling the risk, committing no more than can be delivered, and agreeing to penalties if one or both sides default.

The second phase is when resources, deliverables and prices are committed. It is when the supplier may contract to meet milestones by specified dates and when it defines who does what. At this stage, the margin on the deal can be made or lost, depending on whether the negotiation process is managed and controlled professionally. Increasingly, major organizations train or employ professional negotiators to handle their contractual agreements. This is not just to ensure that those organizations get the best possible deal; it is because negotiation has become a highly specialized branch of the selling process, with its own series of techniques and ploys. A good negotiator will understand the process of which he is a part, and will understand when co-operation is appropriate and when confrontation is needed.

Approaching any deal negotiation, the negotiator will have certain objectives. These can be represented by the upper oval in Figure 10.2. The client will also have objectives, which are represented by the lower oval. The area of intersection of the objectives is the 'common ground' between the two. The common ground is the area of co-operative working, where objectives are aligned, and which reflects why one solution is selected as more appropriate than another.

The negotiation process should start by identifying as much common ground as possible. The supplier should define its own objectives and ask the client what its objectives are. It should define the assets that it has that the client wants, and the assets that the client has that the supplier wants.

Handled properly, this can be a positive way of building trust at the outset, an important pre-requisite if the negotiation is to proceed to a successful conclusion. Understanding of each other's position at an early stage can lead to a more productive negotiation, with more

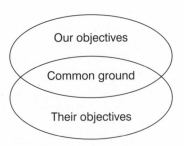

Figure 10.2: *Negotiation approach*

reasoned debate on both sides. Disagreements should, at this stage, be put to one side, whilst both sides build on those things on which they can agree.

At the end of this process, the basis of an agreement will exist. The common ground will have been identified and two other lists of demands will have been drawn up – those objectives and assets that the supplier wants, but the client does not, and those objectives and assets that the client wants, but the supplier does not. The next process is to see how many of these items can be traded into the area of common ground.

Positions and needs

Trading is a critical part of the negotiation phase. Identification of possible trades requires an understanding of the reasons why the client is making the demands that it is making. Similarly, the client needs to understand what the supplier wants. Both sides need to think flexibly and creatively, focusing on the client's needs rather than on stated positions.

Position-stating can kill a negotiation. Interests, by contrast, can be addressed, as the example on page 143 from the Global Life case study indicates.

Plenty of patience and imagination will be required during this stage of negotiations. In the example on page 143, a solution is found to address Global Life's needs, but after their real needs have been understood, rather than by looking at their stated position.

Negotiators who consistently state positions are not just poor negotiators; they also fail to understand the nature of the process in which they find themselves. In any negotiation, both sides have a responsibility to explain to the other what they really want out of the agreement, and this should be done in sufficient detail to allow the fashioning of a sensible negotiated deal suitable to both parties. Negotiators who focus purely on their own needs risk losing out themselves, as this can make finding an optimal win-win much more difficult.

Value and cost

In establishing possible trades, it is important to think of assets in terms of value to the other party, rather than cost. In preparing for a negotiation, it can be easy to under-estimate the value of strong competencies. The client may be attracted to the vendor for many reasons – reputation, experience, financial stability, leading-edge skills. Many of these capabilities will be very important to the client, though they may be of little cost to the vendor.

Every item has a cost to the supplier and a value to the client, or a cost to the client and a value to the supplier. Have a look at the case study detailed at the bottom of page 143.

POSITIONS AND NEEDS

'Global Life Insurance could not possibly agree to slipping the start of code testing to March'

This is Global Life's 'position'. We now need to understand why Global Life could not possibly slip the start of full systems testing until March.

Let us assume that their 'need' is that they have committed to their institutional shareholders that the new system would go live on 1 July. Global Life have remembered that we, in our proposal, suggested at least six months of full systems testing prior to going live. They have therefore concluded that slipping final systems test to March will compromise the project deadline.

We can explore options to address the 'need'. For instance, it may be practical to propose splitting the testing into two three-month periods. Testing of the first phase of code could start in January, in parallel with development of the phase two code. This would allow for a shorter final systems test starting in March, still allowing for a full implementation by 1 July.

VALUE AND COST

Global Life would like access to some of International Consulting's knowledge capital. They are particularly interested in understanding the business process re-engineering experiences that other insurance companies have had following implementation of a new back office.

This information is of a high value to Global Life, as they are unsure of the scale of business process re-engineering the new system will enable them to undertake. Even if they were able to collect the information, interpreting it in the Global Life environment would again prove difficult for them. However, it is relatively easy for International Consulting to collect and analyse this information from their client base.

Accordingly, International Consulting agrees to sell an additional piece of work to produce a report outlining the savings that Global Life will be able to make following the implementation of their new back-office system, and based on similar experiences across their clients in the insurance industry.

International Consulting gets an agreement to produce the report, as an addition to the main contract. Global Life agrees to pay an additional $150,000 for it.

International Consulting has an asset that is worth much to Global Life: namely, the experiences of other insurance companies implementing back-office systems. It will cost International Consulting very little to access that knowledge, but it has a high value to Global Life. Rather than giving Global Life the raw data, International Consulting takes the opportunity to re-package the information in a form that is more useful to Global Life. International Consulting then sells the report as profitable additional business, charging Global Life less than it would cost them to do the work themselves. This is an example of *trading* a low-cost, high-value asset, rather than giving it away.

Game theory revisited

In the process outlined, in defining the common ground, both sides are looking for the win-win territory. During this phase of the negotiation, they are playing a co-operative game. This win-win area is the motivation that is driving them to work together.

Each has something the other wants. In our case study, at the simplest level, Global Life Insurance wants a new back-office system, and International Consulting wants their money. To this end, we decided to work together. This is the start of our common ground.

However, once trading of assets starts, the parties move to the non cooperative element of the negotiation. Here, they are endeavouring to build new win-win territory, or at least territory on which they can agree, by trading or bartering. Whilst the stated positions of each side might be in conflict, examining alternative options that address needs can often lead to ways of building on the common ground already established.

Negotiation is both a zero-sum and non zero-sum game. When objectives are aligned, it is non zero-sum. When they are in conflict, it is zero-sum. The skill of the negotiators is needed to build on the non zero-sum core agreement in order to reach an agreement that covers the largest possible area

BATNA

This chapter has focused on the need to build during a negotiation, rather than to spoil. However, there is always a point beyond which any organization is not prepared to go in a negotiation. Fisher, Ury and Patton (1981) state that neither party should agree to anything that is not as good as their BATNA – their 'best alternative to a negotiated agreement'. In our case study, an example of International Consulting's BATNA is illustrated on the following page.

Possible alternatives to a negotiated agreement include the 'walk-away' choice on either side. For the supplier, this is usually the only

---

INTERNATIONAL CONSULTING'S BATNA

Global Life has requested a discount of 20 per cent on International Consulting's quoted standard consultation rates. However, International Consulting has, after a detailed internal financial review, decided that it does not want the work unless it can negotiate a discount of less than 15 per cent. The negotiator has been instructed to walk away from the deal if Global Life cannot be persuaded to accept a discount of less than 15 per cent.

International Consulting is therefore not prepared to negotiate a deal at or above the 15 per cent discount rate, and would prefer the alternative of not doing the work at all if this cannot be negotiated; walking away from the deal when the discount rate is 15 per cent or more is therefore their best alternative to a negotiated agreement, or their BATNA.

---

alternative. For the client, the range of alternatives is wider and could include the following:

❑ selection of another supplier;
❑ re-opening of the tender process;
❑ re-evaluation of the programme or project;
❑ seeking a different approach.

On coming to a negotiation, the supplier should always have a clear idea of its BATNA, otherwise it risks entering into an agreement that it does not want. Before starting, it should also endeavour to discover, or at least guess at, the client's BATNA. This should give a good feeling as to whether there is the making of an agreement, or whether the forces that are pulling the two sides together (defined by the common ground) are weaker that those separating them. No company should be afraid to walk away from *bad* business, but it should not stop in its quest for innovative approaches to resolve issues at the negotiation stage.

SUMMARY

An understanding of the underlying principles at play in a negotiation, and of how it is meant to work, is essential. In practice, however, margins can be won and lost in the heat of an intense negotiation. The next chapter looks at the practice of negotiating – how to prepare, the tricks and ploys to look out for, and the behaviours to avoid.

Understanding the theory is vital, but putting the theory into practice is what really makes for a successful negotiation.

KEY POINTS

- Understand our objectives and those of our client.
- Understand our own assets and BATNA; estimate the client's.
- Build on common ground.
- Trade flexibly and creatively.
- Focus on needs, not positions.

11

NEGOTIATION PRACTICE

When a man tells me he's going to put all his cards on the table, I always look up his sleeve.

Lord Hore-Belisha, Secretary of State for War, 1937–1940

INTRODUCTION

Over recent years, I have run many types of sales-training workshop for clients. One of them deals with negotiation skills, and it starts with a fairly simple negotiation game. The participants are split into two teams. Each team is given a written briefing and they are given time to prepare for a negotiation with the other side. The negotiation itself lasts about half an hour. Whilst each side has very different objectives, usually some level of agreement is found. At the start of the debrief following the negotiation, I write down on a flip chart what has just been negotiated.

I have run the game about fifty times and have witnessed something quite remarkable. Working with identical briefs, in similar surroundings, no two teams have ever reached the same agreement. On one occasion, two teams of lawyers failed to achieve anything and simply heaped abuse upon each other from entrenched positions. A group of salesmen achieved a comprehensive agreement, but gave away so much that they risked bankrupting their organization. On many occasions, some very strong and comprehensive agreements were reached. There are clearly variables at play in a negotiation that transcend pure logic or inhibit the finding of 'the perfect solution'. Those variables are the people themselves. Personality, behaviour and skill can either make or break negotiations.

This chapter discusses some of the techniques available to the negotiator, to enable him to navigate through the minefield of a negotiation and perhaps avoid some of the more obvious pitfalls.

STRUCTURE

Any negotiation has five phases, represented by the mnemonic 'POETS' – Prepare, Open, Explore, Trade, Settle (Figure 11.1).

Prepare

Preparation for any sales activity usually offers a rapid payback. To negotiate successfully, preparation is essential – objectives need to be defined, and the supplier must also decide what assets it wants from the other side. This will define the 'ideal position', or the starting point in the negotiation. An element of realism is important. Making a 50 per cent wage demand might be a theoretical 'ideal', but it is unlikely to be credible with negotiators working for an employer. Putting such a demand forward is likely to undermine the negotiator's own credibility, both with those with whom he is negotiating and with his own side. It can easily generate an equally unreasonable starting position on the other side. Such an unreasonable demand could even prevent a negotiation from starting at all.

Defining the starting position will depend upon many factors: how badly the vendor wants the business, the strength of its negotiating position, the other options it has. Erring on the side of caution is also a mistake, as this will mean that there is less to trade with once the common ground has been established.

The 'ideal' position should, therefore, be the best position that can be credibly defended as reasonable. It should comprise a list of what the negotiator would like to get from the negotiation. In generating this list, consideration needs to be given to all the major issues, including those that have already been agreed. The list should also be grouped according to those things that are critical and those that are less important.

The negotiator should endeavour to do the same for the client – estimate what its ideal position is likely to be and what is most important to it, and think what assets the negotiator has that the client will want.

Having established the ideal position, and having guessed that of the client, the BATNA of each should then be estimated. For the seller, BATNA represents the 'walk point': the point at which further compromise during the negotiation will yield a solution that is less attractive than walking away. An attempt should also be made to assess the alternatives open to the buyer, should the negotiation fail. Done properly, this will indicate whether there is a good chance of achieving an agreement

Figure 11.1: *Phases of a negotiation*

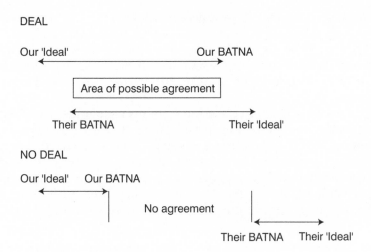

Figure 11.2: *Establishing whether a deal can be struck*

or not, as illustrated by Figure 11.2. If there is a large area of possible agreement across all issues, there is likely to be plenty of room for trading, and a good agreement for both sides should be achievable. If there is no area of possible agreement, the supplier needs to be prepared to walk away from the negotiation. Of course, it is essential to check very thoroughly that the situation has been read correctly, and that there is really not enough common ground, but, ultimately, no agreement is better than a bad agreement.

At this point, the supplier should have a clear idea of what it wants, what it thinks the client wants, what is important to both sides, where they are likely to agree, and where they are likely to disagree. The supplier should have a good idea of whether there is a basis for an agreement. Summarize these preparations by writing them down. It acts as a useful reminder, is a good tool for briefing others, and can be used for internal review.

Operational preparations

How the negotiation will be run is also an important aspect of preparation. For a conclusion to be reached, the right people need to be lined up, with sufficient authority to commit their organization. The lower the number of people involved on each side of a negotiation, the more focused the discussion is likely to be. A recipe for a protracted negotiation is one involving lawyers, accountants, experts for this and that, and line managers. A single decision-maker on each side is likely to give a simpler and quicker result. It is, however, part of the very nature of major deals is that most negotiations are protracted and complex, with many different parties demanding a presence at the negotiating table.

If each side is to field a negotiating team, team discipline is important. A word out of place by a well-meaning team member can create havoc with a negotiating position. The case study below is not untypical.

Every member of the negotiating team needs to understand the negotiating team's strategy, and his particular role in the negotiation. Meeting etiquette between team members needs to be established beforehand. One way of managing the process is to agree that the team leader has total control and that team members only contribute to the dialogue when invited to do so by that lead negotiator. This approach can work if the negotiation is very formal, if the teams do not know each other well,

---

'HELP' FROM AN EXPERT

International Consulting was in trouble and wanted to set up a trade with Global Life.

In exchange for producing an additional piece of computer code outside the agreed scope of the contract, International Consulting wanted to slip delivery of the entire programme by a month. Unknown to Global Life, International Consulting was behind schedule with coding other parts of the system and needed the slippage, whilst Global Life wanted the extra code. There appeared to be the making of a deal.

Global Life was at first receptive to the proposal, but was unsure whether the trade was suitably balanced on both sides. International Consulting's negotiator was insistent that it was.

'Production of the code will take us at least a month,' he claimed. 'It will need to be designed – 1 week – written – a second week – integrated with the existing code – a third week – and tested fully – a fourth and final week. We need to slip the entire programme a month.'

There was silence whilst Global Life considered this point. There was an element of tension in the room. It became too much for one of International Consulting's technical experts, who had been brought into the negotiation at the last minute to advise on detailed technical issues. Not understanding the game plan that was being played out, he made a suggestion.

'Excuse me,' he piped up from the far end of the negotiating table, 'but we could easily cut the code and get it installed in less than two weeks if it were needed that fast.'

Global Life's suspicions were confirmed. International Consulting's negotiating position was undermined. Global Life refused to slip the project more than two weeks. International Consulting had to bring in significant additional resources to meet the revised programme schedule.

Lack of team discipline had cost International Consulting the initiative in the negotiation process and had also cost them a lot of money.

---

or if the negotiation is confrontational. However, once negotiating teams have got to know each other better, negotiations can become more informal and, therefore, less easy to control. An approach to managing this situation is to break out the teams into smaller functional discussion units, getting lawyer to talk to lawyer, and accountant to accountant, for example. Any unresolved functional issues can then be referred back to the lead negotiators to discuss. This way, the ultimate decision-making authority is retained by the lead negotiators, whilst the more detailed issues are thrashed out at a lower level.

The seating plan can make a lot of difference to the atmosphere of a negotiation, and thought needs to be given as to how best to arrange the participants. If the objective is to break down barriers, an informal environment can be created; to encourage co-operative working, mixing up the negotiating teams can be effective. One approach is to sit the two lead negotiators next to each other, and then pair off experts with similar areas of interest, seating them side by side. It is much more difficult to argue aggressively whilst sitting next to someone, and the breaking up of the tribal identities of each team can be helpful in reaching consensus. If both sides are lined up as teams, in opposition to each other across the negotiating table, confrontation is invited.

The major drawback to mixing up the negotiating teams around the table is that the lead negotiator may have less control. Inevitably, individuals with similar problems will tend to want to talk to each other about their area of the negotiation; properly managed, this can be an effective approach both to negotiation and to relationship-building. If this approach is to be followed, it can help to run formal sessions, where strict discussion protocols are observed, with the team leaders doing most of the talking, setting the guidelines, and defining the broad principles and parameters within which the deal must fall. These formal sessions can be interspersed with protracted breaks, or break-out sessions, when individual pairs of negotiators with similar interests can then discuss their areas of responsibility, within the context of the overall negotiation.

Another aspect of preparation relates to the people themselves. The importance of personality type has already been discussed. Matching negotiators of a similar personality type will inevitably oil the wheels of the negotiation machine. If one negotiator wants to continually delve into the minutest detail, whilst the other wants to get the broad principles established first, conflict and suspicion can grow. If the first round of a negotiation has gone badly, consideration of the personality of the players might throw some light on the situation. To make progress on round two, it may be appropriate to modify the style or, in extreme circumstances, to change the negotiator for one better suited to the personality type of the other side.

The organizational levels of the negotiating individuals are important and should be matched as closely as possible. If side A fields its managing director whilst side B fields a salesman, side B is at a distinct advantage. Side A will carry all its authority into the negotiation, whilst side B will only be able to agree to terms, subject to the agreement of the top management. This will enable side B to draw out side A's BATNA, whilst not committing its own negotiating position – an advantage that side A would be naive to allow. For this reason, before a serious negotiation starts, both sides need to sit down and agree who from each side will participate. Every effort should be made to balance the authority levels as closely as possible, if healthy and productive discussions are to proceed in an atmosphere of trust and co-operation.

Open

Preparations have been completed and day one of the negotiation has arrived. Both sides are seated around the negotiating table, ready to open the negotiation.

It is likely that there will be some tension in the air. Negotiations are invariably confrontational to a degree and the anticipation of confrontation is often more nerve-racking than confrontation itself. But tension can be counter-productive and both sides should have an interest in reducing it at the start.

One side will usually assume administrative control of the meeting; this will usually be the buying side. A good start can be made by asking each person to introduce himself to the meeting and explain the reasons why he is there, the interests that he has, and where he expects to contribute to the agreement. If the leader of each team assumes responsibility for bringing in each member of his own team, his position of authority and leadership can be quickly established in the eyes of the other team.

Relationships and attitudes can be established early and first impressions often stick. Showing interest in and respect to the other speakers at this stage will make an impact around the table. Respect is usually mutual: if you show respect to someone, they will usually reciprocate; conversely, if you ignore or belittle someone, they are unlikely to forget it quickly.

Next, agreeing what needs to be achieved should be tabled. A clear articulation of the overall objective, agreed by both parties at the outset, gives the negotiation purpose and direction. The objective should be phrased positively.

Threats should be avoided at all costs. A statement such as, 'If we do not get the price we want, I guess we will have to call the deal off,' will serve no useful purpose at this stage. It will do little to strengthen a negotiating position, tending to harden attitudes on the other side and decreasing the likelihood of an agreement.

Finally, some sort of outline agenda for the day and for the rest of the negotiation needs to be agreed. Logistics such as coffee breaks, lunch, break-out sessions and secretarial facilities for the visiting team need to be clarified and communicated.

Explore

The preparations completed, the preliminaries over, both sides are now ready to start exploring the other's position. Remember that, whilst each knows its own, they have only guessed at each other's. They are in the same boat and therefore some exploratory work is useful to both parties at this stage.

One way of doing this work is to use a white-board approach. Take two differently coloured pens. Invite the teams to make two lists: all agreed items in one colour, and those items that need to be debated in another colour. This process can be used productively by both parties, to gauge the other side's views; if it is done properly, both sides can gain a fuller understanding of the overall picture. It can also be used to establish the common ground.

During this phase of the negotiation it should become apparent whether there is the basis of an agreement between the two parties. However, effort on both sides will be needed, to ensure that a positive exchange of views is maintained. When conflicting interests are at stake, emotions and temperament can get in the way of productive debate. It is important not to rise to the bait if one side indulges in point-scoring, personal attack, interrupting, or sarcasm, and to avoid responding in like tone to such abuse. Cycles of attack and defence invariably drive a wedge between parties. Relationships and trust can quickly be undermined, and, once this happens, finding that elusive win-win territory becomes much more difficult. Mutual trust is the basis of winning a co-operative game. Provocation, insulting language, failing to listen to the other side and personal abuse serve no purpose other than to undermine and, ultimately, destroy a negotiation. Such behaviour is pointless if a negotiated agreement is genuinely sought by both parties.

Having established the common ground and the areas of disagreement, both sides should endeavour to understand what the other side is seeking and why. Getting to the needs behind the stated positions is crucial if effective trades are to be established. Needs can be addressed with creative proposals, whereas positions cannot; see page 154.

My mother gave me some good advice when I was a youngster: 'You have two ears and one mouth. Try using them in that proportion.'

As with most aspects of selling, at this stage, remembering to listen is important. It can be a natural instinct to want to get your own position across, and listening to what the other side wants can be frustrating. This instinct needs to be suppressed and overcome. Only by understanding the other side's needs will the negotiator be equipped to find options that suit both sides in the final agreement.

Good questioning technique is a powerful aid at this exploratory phase of the negotiations. Open questions can be used to encourage the other side to talk and, therefore, allow the negotiator to gain a better understanding of their position. Open questions offer the respondent an opportunity to open up. An example of an open question might be, 'What is Global Life looking to achieve during this negotiation?'

Conversely, closed questions, negative responses or challenging remarks can cause the other side to clam up. An example of a closed question might be, 'Does Global Life want a fixed price for this work?' Closed questions usually invite a binary response. Encouragement and remaining positive are the key to the successful execution of the exploration phase.

Trade

An Arctic explorer, crossing the ice with his huskies and sled, was chased by a pack of wolves. To distract them, he threw them some meat from his

---

POSITIONS AND NEEDS

Global Life's negotiator has stated his position on the code delivery timetable: 'Our position is that we will not slip the deadline for delivery of the phase 1 code beyond the end of March next year.'

International Consulting knows that such a deadline is impractical, so its negotiator asks, 'What is the significance of the March deadline to Global Life's business?'

Global Life responds: 'We have cash available in this year's budget that we wish to spend on this phase during this financial year.'

International Consulting checks whether there are any operational reasons for needing the code in March, to which Global Life says there are not.

Now understanding the need behind the stated position, International Consulting suggests the following:

'We will both be exposed in delivering the full phase 1 code by the end of March. There could be considerable disruption if we were to rush to complete early and release faulty code to Global Life. If we were to offer to take early payment from you at the end of March, whilst committing to phase 1 delivery by the end of April, then what would we have to do to ensure that your needs were fully protected after we had received payment?'

---

stock of much-needed provisions. The wolves devoured it all, then gave chase again. He repeated the action, and again the wolves pounced on the food and ate the lot. Eventually, he threw away the last of his meat, and the wolves consumed it all. When they caught up with the sled, they devoured the explorer.

In negotiations, it is a well-known maxim that a negotiator should never give something for nothing. Do not assume that giving something will encourage the other side to give anything back; they may behave like the wolves. The best way to make progress is by bartering, or trading.

The trading phase of the campaign can be the most difficult to execute successfully. Individuals may resist compromising their stated position for several reasons: they may not be authorized to move; they may see it as a sign of weakness; there may be personal tensions and antagonism between the negotiating parties. Yet, as long as two parties are still present at the negotiating table, the opportunity to find a solution and to strike a deal remains. The fact that both parties are still at the table indicates that there is still some give in both parties' positions; both are clearly prepared to bend in certain areas in order to win an agreement. This means that the negotiator needs to be on the look-out for signals that offer a willingness to trade, and also needs to offer signals himself.

Signals that a party is prepared to trade usually take the form of offering or hinting at a change or softness, but only in exchange for a 'give' from the other side. Willingness to trade could be identified from such statements as, 'Our usual terms for doing business are . . .' (inferring that there are other terms available under the right circumstances); or, 'I cannot personally commit to that . . .' (designating the negotiator's limit of authority, but implying that a higher level of management might be prepared to move); or, 'I cannot agree to that price under these conditions . . .' (implying that it might be possible under modified conditions).

In each of these instances, it is important for the receiving negotiator to recognize that flexibility is being shown or offered, and to encourage it, rather than ignore it. At the very least, thanking someone for making their position clearer is a good idea. Ignoring or slapping down offers of flexibility is unlikely to encourage such behaviour again.

Having established areas of possible trade, a conditional statement can be used, to test them for acceptability. Examples might be: 'If we were to put two extra people on to the change-management project, would you be prepared to slip milestone 3 by a month?'; or, 'The target date you want us to hit for milestone 5 does not currently seem achievable. However, we are prepared to apply extra resource to achieve it. In that event, we would expect some form of bonus payment for meeting it.'

Note that conditions are being traded here. The negotiator is sounding out the client, in order to understand where there is room for manoeuvre and where there is none. Confrontational or threatening statements tend to be counter-productive at this stage. Saying things like 'We could not possibly entertain doing that,' or 'You must be joking if you want us to commit to that,' will only alienate the client and will be seen as posturing by experienced negotiators. If they are asking for something, it must be taken in good faith that that is what they want. In return, the negotiator for the vendor should try to extract a concession or condition that the vendor wants.

Having made a proposal, listen to the reaction. Silence may ensue whilst the other side takes in and considers the suggestion. Do not interrupt. Listen to the response carefully and attempt to respond positively to any further suggestions made.

If, during a negotiation, there is uncertainty about whether to commit to a suggestion, take time out to consider it, rather than rejecting it out of hand. If it does not exactly fit your requirements, the central idea needs to be developed to meet those requirements better. If the proposal is not entirely clear, play back what you think you have heard in your own words, and ask for corroboration of your understanding. Avoid, if possible, an unqualified 'no'. If an idea has to be rejected, it will be helpful to the other side to explain why certain elements cannot be accepted, and to see if the suggestion may be used in another way.

During the trading process, frequent summaries are a good idea. They clarify to all parties what has been agreed and act as a reminder of what has already been achieved. A simple co-signed minute of what has been agreed is always a good idea at the end of a session, and it is always good practice upon resumption of negotiations to give an accurate summary of those agreed elements.

Creativity and flexibility during the trading phase of the negotiation are important. Sometimes, ideas need to be teased out, as people formulate their thoughts and shape their ideas. But new ideas are vulnerable and fragile – they need careful nurturing and support if they are to develop to fully-grown propositions. Both sides have a responsibility to build constructively on new ideas and thoughts, in the cause of finding agreed common ground. Good negotiators listen to the other side, understand their needs as well as their own, retain an open mind, and build on the positive.

Settle

All negotiators are under pressure. The greatest of these is to reach an agreement or settlement. By the time serious negotiations get under way, there is usually a strong expectation of an agreement. Deciding when to call a halt to negotiations and settle for what is on offer, can be tricky.

It is tempting to hang on in the expectation or hope of obtaining further concessions. This applies, of course, to the other side, so one sensible parameter to assess throughout is the respective strength of each side's negotiating position. If you have just won a major concession for little give, it might be good to quit whilst you are ahead. However, appearing to settle too early can send a signal to the other side that they have given too much, which might cause them to react adversely. It is a good tactic to make the other side believe that any concession has not been given lightly. It makes the client feel good that they have extracted a condition of some worth, and it helps counter-balance the scales in the supplier's favour for any subsequent trading. The win-win is achieved when both sides return to their fold looking good and feeling good about the deal.

There are several tried and trusted ways of concluding a negotiation. The most common, and least risky, is to close the negotiation by summarizing what has been agreed. This should include outlining the trades that have been agreed and the shifts in positions that both sides have made, and emphasizing the benefits to both parties of the resulting settlement.

An alternative, more ambitious close is to suggest one final concession, in exchange for finalizing the agreement. This approach has its dangers; if it fails to close the deal it has failed in its objective, whilst the concession has been declared, thereby damaging the strength of the negotiating position. This approach should only be tried if a summary close fails.

A less satisfactory approach, which can be effective when dealing with bureaucracies, is to suggest a time-out, to allow each side to consider its position. This might typically be a few days. To execute this, a good summary of the positions at the start, and of the progress made, can set the scene for both sides to reflect on that progress, and on whether the agreement is substantive enough to be drawn to a close. It allows for consultation with colleagues and, perhaps, with higher authority, before making a final decision.

A final approach to closing a negotiation is to offer the other party two or more alternative options from which to choose – this is particularly useful when you have aired a couple of ideas for possible inclusion in the final settlement, but cannot afford to offer both.

Examples of these four approaches to settling a negotiation are given in on page 158.

CONCLUSION

In a perfect world, an understanding of the theory and practice of negotiation would be the end of the matter. However, in the real world,

SETTLEMENT APPROACHES

International Consulting: 'We think that we have now reached agreement on the broad issues. Perhaps we can summarize. We started by suggesting that we offer you our services at our average corporate daily rate of $1500, and we estimated the workload to be approximately 175 man years of work. This would have yielded a contract value of $50 million for us. You suggested that, for such a large commitment of work, a discount beyond our normal rates was appropriate. In exchange for a 10 per cent discount on our daily rate, you agreed to commit to an expected spend of $45 million, and to guarantee a spend of $40 million . . .

SUMMARY SETTLEMENT
'. . . We then agreed to carry the risk of any possible over-runs by performing the work for a fixed price of $47 million. I suggest we use that agreement as the basis for drawing up a memorandum of agreement, from which detailed contract negotiation can start.

CONCESSION SETTLEMENT
'. . . However, I note that you are keen for us to assume a higher level of contractual commitment than our usual Time and Materials terms. In the interests of reaching an agreement, we are prepared to commit to perform the entire project for a fixed price of $47 million and to carry the full delivery risk ourselves, but only if we have a tight and unambiguous functional specification.

TIME-OUT SETTLEMENT
'. . . We understand your concerns about our Time and Materials contract. On the other hand, a price of $40 million would leave us financially exposed. I suggest that we both take away the summary of what we have agreed, and reflect on possible future courses of action for our meeting next week.

ALTERNATIVES SETTLEMENT
'. . . We could either live with what is proposed and bill on a Time and Materials basis, guaranteeing us $40 million, but allowing for over-runs at your risk. Alternatively, we could settle on a guaranteed fixed price of $47 million. Which is more acceptable to you?'

negotiations can be tense, acrimonious affairs. Negotiation is important to the preservation of the bottom line, and nerves can easily become stretched to breaking point. Some larger organizations use professional negotiators, in an attempt to get the most from negotiations. Sometimes these people are offered huge financial incentives to get a good deal for their clients, and this increases even more the pressure under which they are working.

With so much at stake, it is hardly surprising that a variety of tricks of the trade are used by some less scrupulous practitioners. Most are easily countered, once recognized. The following chapter has been written to help corporate salesmen recognize some of the more common negotiating ploys, and suggests approaches to handling them.

KEY POINTS

- Plan any negotiation carefully.
- Ensure the opening sets the right tone.
- Understand and explore the client's needs and interests; search for the win-win.
- Explain our needs and interests.
- Do not give away our assets, trade them.
- Do not settle outside our BATNA.

12

NEGOTIATION PLOYS

If you can bear to hear the truth you've spoken
Twisted by knaves to make a trap for fools . . .

Rudyard Kipling (1865–1936), writer and poet

INTRODUCTION

The employee–manager relationship is frequently tested in business, sometimes having to endure tension on a daily, even an hourly basis.

I recall one employee coming to me to request a change of sales territory. He had failed to develop his patch in the preceding year and wanted to take advantage of development work done in other territories by some of his more committed colleagues.

'I can't switch territories within my own region mid-year,' I explained. 'That would be unfair to the other salesmen. However, if you believe there is no potential in your existing patch this year, you could take a six-month project in our education department.'

He was horrified. Salesmen were exceptionally well paid and he knew that taking a staff job in education would mean a considerable loss of earnings, however poor his sales performance. Furthermore, the education department was under-staffed, for a good reason – nobody wanted to work there. The work was seen as repetitive and low-profile.

'Oh, I guess I'm not that keen to change course yet,' he muttered, and shuffled out of my office.

I had used a well-known negotiating ploy referred to by Kennedy as 'The Russian Front' (Kennedy, 1992). I had presented him with a highly unattractive alternative, so that almost any other course of action was acceptable, including staying in the territory from which he was trying to escape.

Ploys are about power. They are manipulative techniques used to alter the power balance between the parties to a negotiation. If one party has power over another, that power can be used to improve that party's lot in the negotiation process. For example, if a buyer has the option to buy from another company, that fact may be used to persuade another supplier to reduce its prices.

USING PLOYS

Nobody likes to be manipulated and ploys are designed to do just that. As a result, many ploys are designed not to appear as ploys at all, but are concealed as something else. Often, the individual being manipulated will not know whether the ploy is real or a bluff. How the ploy is countered will depend on the individual judgement of the negotiator. Effective handling of ploys depends a lot on the relationship between the negotiators and the trust that exists between them.

Using ploys is very risky. The greatest risk is the (often permanent) damaging of the relationship between supplier and client, to the detriment of both parties. Ploys should therefore only be used with caution by either side. Negotiation in a climate of mutual trickery is enormously difficult, as trust between the parties is destroyed. My advice to salesmen is to use ploys *only* when all else has failed and when the stakes are high. They might be used in response to an attempt by a customer to obtain significantly higher discounts or to threats to break off negotiations.

Although he may only use ploys infrequently, every corporate salesman needs to be aware of them and to watch out for their use. In the hands of ruthless negotiators, ploys can be used with devastating effect to influence the outcome of a deal in their favour.

This chapter looks at some of the ploys that I have encountered. It considers their likely impact and suggests ways of combating them. Finally, this section on negotiation concludes with a few common negotiation do's and don'ts.

THE PLOYS

Escalated authority

As you read this, the following scene is currently being enacted in a car showroom somewhere in the world. The deal has been struck; terms have been agreed; the delivery date has been confirmed. The price, after some haggling, has been tentatively pencilled in. 'I've given up so much on the price, I'll just have to agree it with my manager,' the car salesman is saying, as he leaves with the customer's ink still wet on the deal.

This technique, known as 'escalated authority', is powerful. It can achieve the following for the vendor:

☐ however poor the deal is for the buyer, it conveys the impression that he is getting a great deal, because the salesman cannot authorize it personally; making the buyer feel good about the deal is always good sales practice;
☐ salesman and manager have bought themselves some time to consider whether to agree to the deal; the salesman can still break the agreement, acting on the advice of his manager, whereas the buyer is fully committed;
☐ the manager now has the option of entering the negotiation, perhaps saying that the salesman has overstepped his limit of authority; the manager may change the deal, insisting that it may only go ahead at the price agreed if, say, the buyer also pays for an extended warranty.

Escalated authority is often used in this way, late in a negotiation, because of a side-effect it can cause. The authority of the salesman is undermined and the negotiation is transferred to the manager. As a counter-technique, the buyer can legitimately demand to deal with 'the real decision-maker'. A more confrontational alternative can be to warn the salesman that, if the manager changes one word of the deal, it is off.

In a corporate selling environment, professional standards usually dictate that both sides make clear the limit of their authority as the negotiation proceeds. Such escalated authority processes are in place within most large organizations. The negotiating process will usually be based on a group of working-level negotiators on either side, agreeing what they can within the bounds of their own responsibilities and authorities. Above the working-level team will be an 'escalation executive' on each side. When issues cannot be resolved, they can be 'kicked upstairs' for the escalation executives to thrash out. Inevitably, on these escalated issues, both sides will be operating much closer to their firm's BATNA, and a more senior level of sign-off will be necessary if the deal is to go ahead.

Operating within such a process, negotiators on both sides need to decide what to agree and what to escalate. These decisions need not coincide with the negotiators' actual authorities. Deferring a decision to a senior executive can buy time, or can create trading concessions, which the escalation executive may offer later on. It is good negotiation practice, when in doubt, not to make an instant decision. As long as the technique is not over-used, escalated authority can achieve much for the negotiator.

Call the talking clock

I was sitting in a manager's office, discussing a deal. Finally, the manager said he needed to check the deal with his manager. He asked his secretary to put a call through. The telephone rang a few moments later, and he took the call . . .

'Hello, Bob, yes, sorry to call you, but I have Chris with me and we are putting the final touches to the contract' . . . pause . . . 'Yes, of course, do you mind if I bounce an idea off you?'. . . pause . . . 'Yes, price is an issue. I've said we could probably agree to $3 million as long as we get the concession on damages we discussed' . . . longer pause and the occasional frown . . . 'Well, Bob, I've kind of said we would go along with that price' . . . pause and more frowns . . . 'That puts me in a bit of a spot, Bob'. . . much longer pause . . . 'I hadn't realized things were that tight. No, it's OK, I guess we'll just have to keep working on reducing the scope' . . . pause and much rolling of eyes towards me . . . 'OK, Bob, I'll explain the position to Chris. No, thanks for taking the call. No, we can work with that. Thanks. Goodbye.'

He put the telephone down, and looked at me. 'My manager is not happy, Chris,' he said. 'I have no approval to go beyond a price of $2.8 million on this deal – he's adamant about it.'

Salesmen should always be wary of a situation where they only hear one side of a conversation. In the majority of cases, a call will be perfectly genuine, but occasionally it may be a set-up, designed to convey a difficult message to the salesman. I have even heard of people calling the talking clock and pretending to have a conversation with a manager.

If a senior manager is really influencing the terms of a deal remotely, the salesman should insist on having access to him as part of the negotiation process.

Exposed document

The IT manager of a potential client company ushered a friend of mine to a seat facing her across the desk. She very deliberately opened a file marked 'Confidential'. Although it was upside-down, he could see that the top item was a letter written on headed notepaper from one of his competitors.

'I would love to recommend your proposal,' she said, 'but there are some problems which professional etiquette prevents me from discussing with you during the procurement cycle.' She hesitated, touching the letter on the top of her file. 'I'm going to have to leave you for a moment,' she continued. 'Please make yourself comfortable. I will be back in five minutes. I will ask my secretary to have coffee ready for us when I return.'

My friend thought her intent seemed clear. She wanted him to read the letter from the competitor and neither she nor her secretary would interrupt for five minutes.

As soon as she had left the room, he read the letter. The middle paragraph made chilling reading for him: 'We realize that you are happy with your current suppliers and that it would take a special offer for you to consider replacing their equipment. However, we are keen to establish a presence with a few leading blue chip clients, of which you are one. Accordingly, against your recent invitation to tender, we are offering to supply a bank of disk drives at half price, with a guarantee to buy them back at any time, should you not be entirely satisfied.'

Five minutes later, the IT manager returned with two cups of coffee.

'Now, about this procurement,' she said. 'I would dearly love to find a way of recommending your company's disk drives, but I have to tell you that, right now, I don't have a proposal from you that my board would accept. My suggestion is that we meet again in a few days and, although I shouldn't really allow it, I will accept a back-dated re-bid from you, should you wish to modify your proposals.'

After further exchanges, he left her office, with a commitment to return the following week, having reflected on her comments. He knew and she knew that he had just been subjected to the exposed document ploy.

The first question any salesman should ask in such a situation is whether the document is real or not. My friend had to weigh up whether the letter he had seen really had been written by a competitor or by the IT manager's secretary five minutes before he had arrived. In my experience, there is a high probability that any exposed document is a forgery of some sort, designed explicitly to apply pressure to the firm's vendor of choice.

My friend was inclined to believe that the letter he saw was a fake, for several reasons:

❏ it was not common practice for this competitor to make such offers; there were no reports of similar offers elsewhere in the market; the customer was not a particularly attractive reference;
❏ the IT manager was under considerable pressure to reduce costs but was also conservative and risk-averse; what she really wanted was his bid, at a lower price – 'gold for the price of silver'.

Fairly sure it was a bluff, he considered calling a few friends at the client's office, but judged that that would expose his relationship with the IT manager; he was keen to avoid this. In any case, even if the letter was a fake, he still had to find a way of meeting her need to reduce her IT expenditure. He finally resolved the problem to the customer's satisfaction, after much discussion and negotiation, by re-financing the entire IT installation, allowing a payback over five years rather than four, but still charging the full price for the new disk drives. It reduced the customer's next two years' annual outlay by significantly more than the price of the new disk drives.

Exposed memos and letters are a powerful way of applying pressure to a vendor. They usually cause the vendor to reappraise its bid, which is what the client wants. To that extent, it may be academic whether the memo is real or not; the underlying signal for the salesman is that the client wants the vendor to change its stance.

The best way of responding to an exposed document is to understand the client's underlying problems and needs. The salesman should reflect on why the client is showing the information at all. The following assumptions can be made:

❏ The client wants the vendor's solution (otherwise, why bother with the risk of showing the document?). Probably, the route implied by the revealed document gives the client a problem too, but it would be poor negotiating technique to let the vendor in on that.
❏ The current proposal does not meet the client's requirements.
❏ The revealed document does not indicate the only way forward.

Confronted by such a situation, the salesman is best advised to use it in order to understand the customer's real buyer values better, rather than to match the competitor's offer. Such events can be an opportunity for both sides to explore ways in which a better deal for both parties can be crafted.

Hard man/soft man

In the following case study, the deal has been agreed in principle and work has already started on implementation. Simon, the salesman, thought he already had agreement to the deal from the client. However, the client is still trying to negotiate a further discount. To dig himself out of the problem, Simon has brought in a hard man – Harry, the branch financial controller. The two are operating as a team in a meeting with the Bill, the client's IT manager. The meeting has dragged on for half an hour, when Harry, the hard man, appears to make up his mind . . .

Hard man (Harry): 'There's no point in us signing this deal, Simon. We're losing money on it before we start. I say we pull the plug on the whole thing now.'
Soft man (Simon): 'Well, steady on, Harry, both the client and we have invested an awful lot of time and energy getting this far. I think the client should have a say. What do you think, Bill?'

Client (Bill): 'I say we talk more. Maybe we can find a way around this problem.'

Hard man: 'I see no point in continuing, Bill. Simon has already over-stepped the mark on price discount. I say we drop the deal now, before we start believing in Father Christmas.' Harry stands and starts to pack his bag; the other two exchange helpless glances and sit in silence. 'I have a train to catch. Simon – I cannot support the deal on the table, let alone allow any more gives. We're losing money on it from day 1. It's not in our interest or the client's for us to sign up bad business. As far as I'm con-cerned, we have no deal.' Harry holds his hand out towards Bill. 'I'm sorry to be the bearer of bad tidings, Bill, but I have no option. We are not a charity and that's what you're asking us to become. I hope we can do business some other time. I'll see you later, Simon. I have to go.' Harry leaves to catch his train.

Soft man: 'I'm sorry about that, Bill. He's not usually like that. He must feel pretty strongly that I've gone too far.'

Client: 'I'm not impressed with your financial man, Simon.'

Soft man: 'He's no salesman, that's for sure, but he does have the branch manager's ear. I'm in deep trouble on this deal now, Bill. I can't negotiate on the firm's behalf if Harry doesn't support me. I didn't want this deal to fall apart . . .'

Client: 'Well, I don't want that to happen either! We've already started the design work and I committed your solution to the board two weeks ago.'

Soft man: 'Well, you heard what Harry said. Without his support, I've got real problems getting this deal through.'

Client: 'But you've already agreed to the deal on the table. Surely, as the salesman, *you* commit the company, not the financial guy?'

Soft man: 'Yes, but you wanted further price concessions.'

Client: 'Do you think you could get the existing deal through?'

Soft man: 'I'd have said 'yes' before today's discussion with Harry, but, as I said, he has the branch manager's ear. Maybe if I told the branch man-ager I'd already committed the deal to you, he'd vote in my favour. I just don't know, Bill. I've never seen Harry like that before. I felt sure he'd go along with it . . .'

Client: 'Tell you what. Why don't you talk to your branch manager and sell him the deal we've already got, and I'll see if we can't extend our budget to cover it?'

Soft man: 'I can't think of a better way forward. I'll give it a whirl. Let's talk again tomorrow afternoon, and exchange notes?'

The hard man/soft man ploy uses two or more people to apply pressure to the victim, often to break an impasse. The hard-man stereotype is tough, abrasive and direct; the soft man is gentle, sympathetic and under-standing. The ploy relies upon the assumption that different people react to different personalities in different ways. Some crumble under the onslaught of a hard man and give way, whereas others become defiant and stubborn. Alternatively, a reasoned or softer approach might encourage more sensitive personality types to open up, especially if they have recently been roughed up by a hard man. This ploy can be effective in persuading people to open up, although the hard-man approach may also damage existing relationships, sometimes permanently. Such is the power of the technique that it is often used by police interrogating difficult or uncooperative suspects.

The hard man/soft man ploy is easy to spot. If the client tries it, and the salesman feels intimidated, or is in danger of being charmed into submission, the best counter is to bring additional resources into the negotiating arena. It is not necessarily most effective to match hard man with hard man, and soft with soft, although similar personalities can understand one another well. The objective of the counter is to avoid having the two different personalities operate on one victim, but to force a one-to-one or a two-to-two dialogue.

If a sales team decides to use a hard man/soft man approach, it is always worth considering using an outsider to adopt the hard-man role, whilst the salesman retains the relationship with the client by playing the soft man. In this way, the salesman can work at patching up the relationship after the hard man has done his stuff, as in the example quoted. During my sales career, I sometimes used visiting executives to deliver hard messages to customers. As outsiders, they had less to lose by being more direct and had the added authority that an external perspective can bring. If both sides remained on speaking terms after a confrontation, I would use the same executive again next time. If the relationship was more strained, I would switch to somebody different.

Trial close

I remember negotiating the delivery of a mainframe computer; the meetings with the customer had been endless. It seemed that every time we almost reached agreement, someone thought of yet another requirement that needed to be met. Having handled several 'just-one-more-thing' suggestions, I was confronted by a request that we deliver the equipment a week later than planned, because the IT manager, who wanted to be present when the equipment was installed, had decided to take a vacation. In isolation, it might have been a reasonable request but, in the context of what had preceded it, I felt we were being asked to bend to one too many of the customer's whims.

I told the customer, 'Look, we are only six weeks from the scheduled delivery date. The machine is almost built. If I can find a warehouse for it and defer delivery for a further week, can I assume we will then have a plan we can all sign up to, with no further alterations?' Initially, there was silence. The customer had taken our flexibility for granted and was taken aback by my request. However, after some rumblings and whispered discussion, the IT manager agreed to my request.

I had used a trial-close ploy. These are most often used to bring rambling negotiations to a halt. They work by putting the latest request or demand to one side, unresolved, and testing whether there are still other issues that will need to be addressed. If there are other issues to be resolved, the trial close will usually flush them out. If there are none, the salesman knows what he needs to do to close the deal.

Budgets, schedules and non-negotiable terms

The client had reviewed our proposal and professed himself well pleased with it. Everything was fine, apart from one thing – our bid price was 5 per cent above his budget. Could we find a way of getting within his approved ceiling?

When talking to suppliers, many customers find it difficult or embarrassing to use words that express exactly what they mean. As a result, they invent ways to convey their message in a less confrontational manner. The intent is the same: namely, to apply pressure to the supplier. However, the technique de-personalizes the pressure to an abstract, often arbitrary force. Typical of these are the 'budget' and the 'schedule', handed down to the supplier as if cast in tablets of stone. I have frequently been confronted by statements like the following:

- ❏ 'Our budget has an absolute ceiling of $3 million for this project.'
- ❏ 'We require the system to be operational by 4pm on 17 March.'
- ❏ 'Our terms are non-negotiable.'

In my experience, virtually everything in business is negotiable, including budgets, schedules and non-negotiable terms! Such devices are usually artificial constraints applied to managers responsible for looking after negotiations with suppliers. They can usually be broken, as long as the business rationale for doing so is valid.

The key with any artificial constraint is to understand that it is a guide, not an absolute. In a perfect world, the salesman's proposals should fall within the guides given. However, if an artificial constraint prevents the supplier from making a significantly better proposal, inhibiting parameters should be tested. This should be accompanied by a demonstration of why it is believed that the client's imposition is working against the interests of both parties.

Reverse auction

The auctioneer's role is a familiar one. He or she attempts to obtain from a collection of competing bidders the highest possible price for a given item. The reverse auction is designed to achieve the opposite – the 'auctioneer' or client attempts to obtain the lowest possible price from competing suppliers offering their solutions.

A typical scenario might be as follows: three competitors have offered broadly similar solutions to the client's requirements, but one is 15 per cent cheaper than the other two. The client's auctioneer will ring up the other two companies and explain that their proposals are fine, but their price is 'way out of line' and they need to come down by about 20 per cent to be competitive. If one or other does drop its price by 20 per cent, the first competitor is then called and advised that it needs to drop its price by another 10 per cent to be competitive. This cycle can, and usually does, go through several iterations until the client has driven all parties down to their absolutely lowest price level. At this point, the serious evaluation of options can start.

Responding to reverse auctions is not easy for a salesman. It is a nasty technique to counter, as the buyer has a disproportionately powerful position. Further, the buyer has the ability to distort information, as in the example above. The salesman only has the buyer's word for it as to whether the competition has undercut the bid.

One way of handling a reverse auction is not to play the game, stating that the price bid is a fair one and justifying it on the basis of value and business benefit delivered. Whilst this has a certain professional rectitude to it, it often fails. If the client is at all price-sensitive, another company will usually be prepared to play the game, and they are therefore more likely to win.

An alternative is to participate fully. This should only be contemplated if the following applies:

❑ the supplier's BATNA has not been reached;
❑ you are the lowest-cost supplier, and can go on playing longer than anyone else.

Even if this is the case, this is not a clever approach, as the margin will be squeezed on each iteration of the auction.

Neither of these approaches is likely to be particularly attractive, but there is a third approach. After being contacted by the auctioneer, the initial response should be to give nothing, arguing that the bid already represents best business value. At the same time, the salesman should convey the impression that he will 'test the water' internally, but continue to insist that he does not hold out much hope of a price reduction.

He should also establish from the client when the last moment is for sub-mitting a revised price. Until this time, the salesman should continue to test this deadline which, once reached, should trigger the submission of a new, lower bid. In this way, the number of iterations of the auction is limited and, hopefully, with the deadline past, the competition will have no opportunity to respond.

Of course, an unprincipled client will realize what has happened and may well extend the deadline to allow more auction iterations. This behaviour can be partially insured against by insisting at more senior levels within the organization that the client adheres to due process. Ultimately, however, the client is still very much in control and can always bend the rules to suit its own commercial interests.

After being subjected to a reverse auction, win or lose, the supplier organization should reflect on whether this particular client will, in future, form part of their balanced portfolio of customers. Margins will always be squeezed by such a client and the focus is likely to be price, not value. Suppliers need to evaluate whether this is the type of client upon which they want to build their business in the future.

Plea/personal commitment

I was at my desk in a client's office one day when the services director came in, looking agitated. He was as white as a sheet.

'Chris,' he said, 'I have a real problem. You know that new data-entry system we've signed up for? The shop steward has just walked into my office and threatened a mass walk-out if we implement it.'

We had signed a formal contract to supply the equipment the month before and a handsome commission cheque had recently landed in my bank account. I had been aware for some time of concerns regarding pos-sible industrial action across the administrative grades. The new data-entry system business case did entail some re-deployment of staff but, as far as I had understood, no redundancies. The union had, nevertheless, decided to make an issue of the change.

'What do you want to do about it, George?' I asked.

'We are not keen to have a show-down with the union over this at pres-ent,' he replied. After a pause, he added, 'I know I have no right to ask a favour of you, but would you mind if we tore up the contract – at least for the moment?'

Personal pleas are another weapon in the armoury of the skilled negotiator. They are seldom just personal pleas – they normally affect organizations and the legal commitments into which their officers have entered. That request to me had probably been discussed and rehearsed in detail before the director came to me. The client had selected their agent well: he and I had a good personal and business relationship, and had done a considerable amount of business together in the past.

A sense of perspective is always important when weighing personal pleas. In the overall context of the relationship, the rational salesman should consider the upsides and downsides of a given course of action. In the example given, I was under no obligation to tear up the contract and doing so would hit my pocket. The client had dug itself into a hole and wanted me to bail it out, cost-free. On the other hand, this particular client had placed many millions of pounds' worth of business my way, and planned to continue to do so. In the overall context of the relationship, there was much to lose by failing to help out.

Personal pleas are difficult to rebut, but, if circumstances dictate, effort should be expended on keeping the relationship intact. Under this sort of pressure, I would try to broaden the issue, to make it too big to be solved by a personal favour. An approach to the problem above might have been to indicate that the order had already been entered into the firm's books, that the equipment was already being manufactured, and that the sales team had been paid its commission. I might then have claimed that it was not within my power to cancel the order at this late stage. I could then have brought in other, less personally involved managers to the decision.

Another alternative, and the one I actually adopted, was to be sympathetic to the dilemma, but to seek a quid pro quo. I pointed out the problems the cancellation would cause me personally – namely, the loss of commission. We were able to work out an arrangement entirely satisfactory to both of us: the client cancelled the data-entry equipment, but placed a significantly larger software order single tender with me, to enhance my commission payment. As we both reflected some weeks later over a beer, one good turn deserves another.

If capitulation is the chosen route, remember that a personal plea is first and foremost a ploy. Whilst the relationship will probably be preserved in the short term, the client may also think of the salesman as a soft touch and this may encourage similar behaviour again in the future. Once a salesman has ceased to be able to represent his own and his firm's best interest to a client, a wise manager may judge that it is time to change that salesman's territory.

Closing ploys

Several ploys are used in order to close deals. They are usually employed in the final push to reach an agreement and, whilst they often achieve just that, they should be used with caution.

It can be tempting to resolve an impasse by suggesting splitting the difference between the locked parties, but this should only be entertained if it does not push the deal beyond either party's BATNA. A bad agreement does nobody any favours. Both will resent the final give and neither side will be as emotionally committed to the deal. It is better to have no deal than a bad deal.

An inexperienced negotiator will often attempt to apply arbitrary pressure in a negotiation by placing a deal on the table and adopting a take-it-or-leave-it stance. This may indicate that he has reached his company's BATNA, but it is more likely that he himself is under pressure to resolve the negotiation. Even worse, he may impose a time constraint or a 'now or never' condition, by stating that the deal is only valid for the current meeting.

These positions are just that – positions. They do not explain the underlying interest that is causing the negotiator to take the stance. Instead of reacting to the position, the salesman should ignore the threat and endeavour to understand the underlying interest at stake. By addressing that, enough common ground for a better deal may be found.

NEGOTIATION DO'S AND DON'TS

Chapters 10 and 11 have looked at negotiation theory, game-theory models, and the P-O-E-T-S process. This chapter has studied operational considerations, alerting the potential practitioner to the ploys sometimes tried by experienced negotiators.

The conclusion to this section on negotiation looks at a few practical suggestions on what to do and what to avoid in a negotiation, with a top ten (five of each) of operational 'do's' and 'don'ts'.

Do's
Do build relationships
Remember to preserve relationships during the negotiation. Be prepared to lose face in the short term and always attempt to calm any tension. Be persuasive, professional, calm and polite, but not soft. Remember that respect is usually mutual; if you show your opposite number respect, it will usually be returned. Always listen and attempt to understand the other person's point of view. Observe common courtesies, such as remembering names, being punctual for meetings, and being sensitive to the client's concerns. Do not assume that all negotiation will take place during formal meetings; think about setting up a drink after work, meals out and other social events to enhance the relationship. Create an aura of expertise and quiet authority. If others become difficult or emotional, don't follow their example. Acknowledge their emotion until their adrenalin level drops. Avoid smirking or showing irritation.

Do plan

Every aspect of a negotiation that can be planned before the face-to-face encounter, should be; this will include strategies, objectives, likely lines of argument and objection, BATNAs, ploys, locations, team compositions, seating arrangements and personality considerations. Time spent at leisure, under no immediate operational pressure, thinking through how to manage the entire negotiation process will be repaid with interest in results. Plan, plan, plan, and then plan the negotiation some more. It may not ensure success, but an unplanned negotiation is significantly more likely to fail.

Do clarify

Make sure you understand what is being said to you and that you are understood. It is so easy to miscommunicate meaning or sense by the use of unclear terminology or jargon. The use of consistent terminology can help this process a great deal. Use images, stories and analogies to get points across and to bring your ideas to life. Clarify what the other side is saying by re-phrasing it and playing it back, to ensure concurrence. Ensure they mean what you think they mean. Document areas of agreement.

Do look for win-win

Keep exploring and looking for the win-win. Endeavour to set up quid pro quos in order to enlarge the area of agreement. Use 'if' rather than 'yes' or 'no' to explore options with the other parties. Feed lines to the other side, which they can use within their own organization to sell the deal internally.

Do generate trust

Understand local issues and the client's problems. If you are in a tight corner, never lie. Being found to have lied can permanently destroy credibility. If there are areas behind a façade you do not want to expose, opt instead for omission. Do not over-commit or renege on a previous agreement. If you have to de-commit, be open about it and take personal responsibility for the firm's failings. If you blame others, the client will want to talk with them and not with you.

Don'ts

Don't give assets away

Negotiate assets for concessions on the other side, rather than giving them away. Don't agree to a deal if you don't understand why it is attractive to the other side – you have probably missed something.

Don't get emotional

Emotion is an inhibitor to effective negotiation. The more even the temperature, the more likely a successful outcome to any discussion. If you feel close to losing your composure, take time out to cool down and reflect. Understand why the other party is behaving in a particular way and try to get to the underlying issue.

Don't irritate

It is very easy, in the heat of negotiation, to irritate the other parties. In your desire to get your own points across, it can be easy to switch into 'transmit' mode and pay less attention to receiving. Try to avoid the phrase 'yes, but . . .'. This is usually a fairly transparent way of immediately rejecting what has just been said, usually with an attempt to cap it with a strong counter-point. It is the verbal equivalent of an eye for an eye, and invites retaliation. It is also good practice to avoid interruption, ploys and being patronizing, all of which can be instantly irritating.

Don't push too hard

Do not drive the other side beyond its BATNA and do not agree to a deal worse than your own BATNA. Do not split deals down the middle in order to reach a quick settlement. Easy deals are usually bad deals. Avoid bullying the other side, as this also risks alienating the mildest of people. Negotiation should be based on reasoned and calm consideration of options. If either side has been leant on to include terms to which they do not fully subscribe, that side is likely to lack the total commitment to the final contract that may be needed to deliver a successful project.

Don't assume non-negotiable items are non-negotiable

Deadlines, budgets, schedules and prices are *all* negotiable. If the buyer insists otherwise, he is merely stating a negotiating position, and it is incumbent upon you to understand the interests behind this position. Deadlines can be moved if it is to the benefit of all parties to move them. The astute negotiator will try to show how everyone is better off when a meeting that he cannot make is shifted. Budgets are usually set by one person attempting to control the actions of another in the same organization. It may be possible to alter the budget by approaching the budget-setter with an argument that demonstrates what can be achieved with a budget increase. It is a fact of life that almost everything is negotiable, but very few people bother to test constraints when they are delivered as facts.

KEY POINTS

■ Ploys are techniques to put the other side under pressure; recognize them and counter them, but consider carefully before using them.

■ Do: build and preserve relationships, plan carefully, clarify and document areas of agreement, look for win-win scenarios, endeavour to generate trust.

■ Do not: give assets away, get emotional, irritate, push too hard, assume non-negotiable items are non-negotiable.

13

FINAL THOUGHTS

If I have seen further than others, it is because I have stood on the shoulders of giants.

Letter to Robert Hooke
Sir Isaac Newton (1642–1727), mathematician and scientist

INTRODUCTION

Equipped with the models and theories outlined here, the aspiring salesman should feel better-equipped to take on his role. His world, however, is always changing. This final chapter looks at some of the macroscopic changes that are occurring in the business world, and how these changes are influencing the role of the salesman.

INDUSTRY ORGANIZATION

Some years ago, I worked with a firm that was attempting to sell solutions to the UK Meteorological Office. I arranged for a senior sales executive – I will call him Mr Smith, to protect the guilty – to join one of their managers and me for lunch.

Over the hors-d'oeuvres, the Met man started talking about the use of weather ships in the Northern Atlantic. The ships were old and needed refurbishment. The selling firm had recently developed a state-of-the-art ship-navigation system and Mr Smith at once saw a sales opportunity.

'Have you looked at our ship-navigation system?' he asked. 'It uses leading-edge technology. It increases the productivity of ships by offering you all the controls you need to manage the ship most efficiently. It does automatic course navigation through a gyroscopic compass. It continuously monitors the horizon and, as necessary, brings in appropriate anti-collision software. This is of particular benefit in foggy conditions. Fuel consumption is monitored and optimized for any given journey and you can receive a read-out of your precise location at any moment in time.'

He leant back with a satisfied expression and a triumphant flourish of the hand. We had just witnessed his one-minute sell routine – clinically executed, with all the client benefits highlighted, and delivered with machine-gun efficiency.

The Met man's brow furrowed. He was a naturally polite man and was clearly having difficulty in deciding how to respond. Eventually, he turned to Mr Smith and said, 'Well, that is very interesting, but I don't think it would work for us.' He paused. 'You see, our weather ships don't have engines. They are towed out to fixed moorings at sea and remain anchored there until we go out to collect them. A navigation system would be of little use to them and, of course, being anchored, they consume no fuel. We don't need a location read-out, as the ships are anchored to fixed points, and they and we know exactly where these are. The onus is on other vessels to avoid colliding with our ships.'

There was silence. Not a morsel of our proposal remained, our credibility was shot to pieces. For the rest of the lunch, our conversation retreated to the relatively safe areas of current affairs and the weather. Ignorance of the industry had been our downfall.

To sell complex bids more effectively, most companies now organize their sales operations along industry lines and require their sales people to understand their particular industry. This type of organization has largely superseded geographic- or product-based sales-forces, because a good understanding of the industry's dynamics and problems is necessary for the creation of appropriate solutions. In fact, this requirement is so important that many companies now frequently recruit sales people from those industries to which they wish to sell.

One challenge creeping up on industry-based sales-forces is the blurring of industry lines. UK food retailer Tesco is now also a leading petrol retailer. Twenty years ago, the petrol industry was almost exclusively vertically integrated, with companies such as Exxon, Texaco and Shell controlling the retail outlets. Some petrol companies, meanwhile, have developed their forecourts into mini shopping malls. Marks and Spencer, having started in clothes retailing, now sells food too. It has also moved aggressively into financial services, as have General Motors and some of the utility companies. IBM, ICL, Unisys and Honeywell, once known primarily as technology companies, have all re-branded themselves as services or solutions companies. Virgin started life as a record company, but is now a diverse brand, embracing such industries as drinks, transportation and financial services.

Industries are converging, and the boundaries are blurring. In future, the corporate salesman may need to have a working knowledge of not just one but several industries, if he is to understand and match the needs of the ever-more diversified and sophisticated client.

A GLOBAL VIEW

The race is on to become 'global'. The majority of large businesses are attempting to convince clients that they are more global than their competitors. Global is a vague term that appeals to the egos and aspirations of many senior managers but, when pressed to outline what constitutes a 'global organization', those managers will come up with many different definitions.

I once asked a director of a large chemical company what he meant by his claim to be global. He answered, in all seriousness, that his company was global because it had recently installed a company-wide Lotus Notes e-mail system. To another director in manufacturing, it meant having plant on three different continents. IBM underlines its global aspirations by including the message 'Solutions for a small planet' in its corporate advertising.

Commonly cited prerequisites for a global solution-deliverer include a common product or service line across all countries, a presence and common branding around the world, and an accountability in local managements to resolve issues outside their country or region.

However, in my experience, when clients say they are interested in a supplier's global credentials, they are looking for attributes that are additional to the services offered. International companies buying from a single supplier in many different countries will usually look for some sort of discount based on the aggregate of business transacted across the world. Often, they will look for a single contracting point and a single point of resolution for disputes that occur anywhere in the world. They will look to the supplier to allocate resources from a global resource pool and will need reassurance that the firm has the management processes in place that can allow this to happen. Over and above common product and services around the world, they will look for common processes, quality and after-sales service levels. Having satisfied themselves of the organization's global credentials, they will want a product or service that is personalized and attentive to local market needs, wherever it is delivered to the client. 'Global service/local service' may well become the client's mantra in the next millennium; the capacity to deliver such a service successfully may become the single most significant differentiator between suppliers.

The organizational dynamics, training and logistics necessary to deliver to this agenda are daunting. Probably, no major organization in the world is fully delivering to it yet, although many aspire to it. The race is on and competitive advantage for the early arrivals will be immense.

When dealing with global clients, the corporate salesman needs to understand how much his own organization is capable of delivering to the global ideal and the plans it has to improve in the future. The managements of selling organizations need to understand that, if they want to do business with major multi-nationals in the next millennium, they have to do more than talk about becoming global. They must start taking difficult company-wide management actions in order to re-structure their operations.

The global marketplace is increasingly demanding a service level that really is global.

CONTROL

Military analogies are frequently used to illustrate points to do with selling. Selling is at the front line of most successful businesses and there are many similarities between a military and a sales campaign. Situations are won or lost. A strong line of command and control is necessary if a sales team is to function efficiently. It is critical to choose the right battleground on which to engage the competition, in order to capitalize on one's own strengths and on the opposition's weaknesses. Good teamwork, high morale and determination are important factors in determining success. In short, training and discipline, hierarchy and control, are all prerequisites for the successful operation of a sales team facing the operational chaos of a sales campaign.

These principles, however, do not sit easily alongside modern management thinking. During the 1980s and 90s, much of Western industry was re-structured. Flatter organizations and greater spans of control, empowerment of the workforce and devolved decision-making became the new management imperatives. Implicit in these changes was a loss of control, which had to be compensated for by new technology, increased accountability in the management systems and better business processes.

In my experience, if a sales team is to operate effectively, management discipline is of the essence. Good sales campaigns do not just happen. The lead salesman needs to ensure that every customer contact forms part of an overall sales strategy. He needs to ensure that his firm is conveying a consistent message to all levels of client management. Every client contact should form part of the overall sales campaign strategy. Every client contact should be controlled and authorized by the lead salesman. Every call should be carefully planned. Control is at the heart of a successful sales campaign, and ensuring that control is maintained requires an investment of time, effort and energy.

This is not to criticize creativity, thinking out-of-the-box, or moving the campaign outside conventional processes. As in a military battle, when the situation requires it, an appropriate change in strategy can catch the competition hopping. It can be decisive in executing a winning campaign. However, when a new direction is to be implemented, the entire client-facing team needs to understand it. Maverick 'shooting from the hip' by any member of the sales team can create disastrous disarray within the team itself.

THE ROLE OF THE SALESMAN

Markets and industries will change. Companies and company executives will come and go. New processes and technologies will revolutionize the workplace. New management theories will replace the old. There is nothing so certain as change.

Yet the corporate salesman will always have a role. Large complex deals will always need to be crafted individually, in co-operation with the client. As the complexity and interdependence of corporate business increases, clients will increasingly demand closer business partnerships with their suppliers. The corporate salesman is the cornerstone of such relationships between firms.

Within that context, the primary role of any salesman is to match, as convincingly as possible, his company's capabilities to the client's needs. It sounds straightforward but, in practice, delivering to the brief can prove elusive. In the real world, there is only a finite number of opportunities for the salesman to get his message across. Clients do not always hear, or want to hear, what is being said. Personal agendas and office politics can get in the way of sound business decisions. Clients rarely behave entirely rationally, especially when under pressure. Emotions and instincts often outweigh logic in the final assessment.

At the start of a campaign, the salesman will need to work out how he is going to win the sale. First, he will want to be sure it is the right business for his firm to take on. Senior-management support will be needed during the campaign and, if this is only half-hearted, it will show during the course of the selling activity.

Once the company is committed to making the sale, selecting the right battleground is important. The salesman will want to be able to demonstrate his firm's strengths, and highlight the competition's weaknesses. He will want to differentiate the solution in ways that add real value to the client. He will need to focus his efforts on those three or four critical messages he wants the client to understand and accept in making his evaluations. In the time available, he cannot hope to convey everything he might like to include. Focus and continuous reinforcement of the few most important messages throughout the sales campaign are therefore essential.

A campaign needs tight management. Every call, every presentation, every visit, in fact, every interaction with the client should form part of an overall sales strategy. The salesman needs to understand the influence and power that each client individual will have on the final decision. He will need to focus his efforts on those individuals whom he needs to convince of the solution. Every client contact should form part of the overall battle plan. Each call should be carefully planned and have clear objectives which are in line with the overall campaign strategy.

To be effective, the salesman needs to understand, detect and counter problems raised by the client. He needs to be continuously alert to messages and feedback. Listening, and understanding what the client is trying to communicate, is crucial to success. Often, clients are not overly articulate. In such situations, careful questioning, and a real desire to understand, are invaluable qualities in a salesman.

Having heard and understood the client, the salesman may need to change proposals. Such a decision needs to be carefully weighed. The salesman should endeavour to adapt where possible, or where the cost to his own company is low, but, clearly, saying 'yes' to everything the client asks for is not always practical. Recognizing what the client has requested and sensitively articulating why the firm is unable to acquiesce to those demands needs careful handling. The salesman needs to demonstrate that he has listened to, fully understood and respected the client's advice. These are important precursors to turning down a client's requests.

A salesman represents both his company and himself. To operate successfully, he needs to be able to build and sustain long-term business and personal relationships. Seeing the world and its problems through the client's eyes can help. Adapting behaviour to accommodate the client's personality may be appropriate to ensuring more effective communication. Ensuring that the sales messages appeal to buyer values usually guarantees the client's interest. Phrasing sentences in a way that is sensitive to the client's level in the organization will help make messages more relevant.

Finally, personal qualities of integrity and honesty effectively conveyed to the client are essential to selling success at this level. Corporate selling is about creating a climate of trust between vendor and client, which will extend beyond the buying decision and into delivery of the solution. Complex deals often have an impact upon mission-critical areas of the client's business. In buying a solution, the client will want to believe that the vendor will be there as a partner, ready to support him and solve problems when the going gets rough. The salesman who can best sell himself, and his firm, as a reliable and trustworthy business partner will always have the edge on the rest of the field; he will also be a valuable asset to the firm he represents.

ON THE SHOULDERS OF GIANTS . . .

This book seeks to promote ideas that have been of use to me. I take no credit for many of the models described. Maslow and Mintzberg, Herzberg and Handy are the icons of management theory and giants in their field. My task has been to take their ideas, and those of others, and apply them to a sales environment.

Similarly, the sales-campaign tools discussed, such as power maps, marker lists, SWOTs and others, have been used by salesmen for many years. As a package, they offer a set of aides for the aspiring sales executive, to help him navigate a path through the complex business of managing a major sales campaign.

Most important of all, you, the corporate salesman, need to remember that clients are real people and treat them accordingly. When attempting to close the order, think what *they* will get out of the deal – not what you want. See the world through their eyes. Relate to their perspective. Understand what makes them tick and find a way to give it to them. Paradoxically, giving them what they want is the most effective way of getting what *you* want.

In conclusion, I offer one final piece of advice.

In any field of human endeavour, individuals excel when they enjoy what they are doing. Businessmen or sportsmen never say at the end of a successful career, 'I hated every minute.' Enjoyment and success are symbiotic. Selling is no exception.

A career in selling is inevitably a roller-coaster ride of ups and downs. Learn to enjoy the excitement of the trip. For each sale won, there are usually several lost. Losing can be stressful and energy-sapping, and can lead to moments of despair and self-doubt. The scars of battle can run deep and be personally hurtful. However, it is important to keep such failures in perspective. Learn from them, then forget them. There is still a whole world out there waiting to be sold to, perhaps just waiting to hear from you.

Winning, of course, is much more fun than losing. The exhilaration of that first sale, won, perhaps, against the odds, is unforgettable. Any win, however small, can be personally rewarding. Remember the wins, and revel in them. They are very sweet, and worth waiting for.

Only when you get there will you really understand how very special winning can be.

REFERENCES

Axelrod, R. (1984) *The Evolution of Co-operation*, Basic Books, New York

Fisher, Ury and Patton (1981) *Getting to Yes*, Houghton Mifflin Company, London

Haley U.C.V. and Stumpf S.A. (1989) 'Cognitive Trails in Strategic Decision-making: linking personalities and cognitions', *Journal of Management Studies*, Vol 26, Number 5 (1989) pp 477–97

Handy, C. (1976) *Understanding Organisations*, Penguin Books, London

Handy, C. (1994) *The Empty Raincoat: Making sense of the future*, Hutchinson, London

Johnson, G. and Scholes K. (1988) *Exploring Corporate Strategy*, Prentice Hall, Hemel Hempstead

Kennedy, G. (1992) *The Perfect Negotiation*, Century Business, London

Luft, J. (1969) *Of Human Interaction*, National Press, Palo Alto, California

Maslow, A.H. (1968) *Toward a Psychology of Being*, Van Nostrand Reinhold, New York

Mintzberg, H. (1979) *The Structuring of Organisations*, Prentice Hall, Hemel Hempstead

Myers, I.B. (1987) *Introduction to Type*, Consulting Psychologists Press Inc., Palo Alto, CA 94303

O'Connor, J. and McDermott, I. (1996) *Principles of NLP*, Thorsons, London

INDEX